THEOLOGY & AUTHORITY
Maintaining a Tradition of Tension

Edited by

RICHARD PENASKOVIC

HENDRICKSON
PUBLISHERS
PEABODY, MASSACHUSETTS 01961-3473

ISBN 0913573-77-9

Theology & Authority

To Bill Penaskovic,
who has taught me so much
about life; a brother whom
I shall always respect and
love.

Table of Contents

About the Contributors

Michael H. Barnes holds the Ph.D. in religious studies from Marquette University and teaches religious studies at the University of Dayton. He recently published In the Presence of Mystery with Twenty-Third Publications in Mystic, Connecticut.

David M. Bossman teaches Jewish-Christian studies at Seton Hall University. He received the Ph.D. from St. Louis University and is editor of Biblical Theology Bulletin.

James M. Dawsey received the Ph.D. from Emory University, teaches New Testament studies at Auburn University, Alabama, and recently penned The Lukan Voice, published by Mercer University Press, 1986.

Jo Ann Eigelsbach has a Ph.D. in religious studies from the Catholic University of America. She is a member of the American Academy of Religion Working Group on Roman Catholic Modernism and the Lonergan Workshop. Her publications include, "The Intellectual Dialogue of Friedrich von Hügel and Wilfrid Ward," in The Downside Review.

James Heft, S.M. (Marianist), received his Ph.D. in historical theology from the University of Toronto. He currently chairs the Religious Studies Department at the University of Dayton. His book, John XXII and Papal Teaching Authority was published by the Edwin Mellen Press in 1986.

Wayne Hellmann completed his doctoral studies at the Ludwig Maximilians University of Munich with a dissertation on the concept of "ordo" in St. Bonaventure. He has written for, and served as an editor of Theology Digest. He finds himself most at home in Franciscan studies and teaches in the Department of Theological Studies at Saint Louis University.

Brennan Hill took a degree in English from Cambridge University in addition to receiving the Ph.D. in religious studies from Marquette University. He has written six books and numerous articles in the field of religious education. Presently, he teaches theology at Xavier University in Cincinnati.

Ronald D. Pasquariello is Senior Fellow for Urban and Economic Policy at the Center for Theology and Public Policy, Washington, D.C. He received the Ph.D. in religious studies from the Catholic University of America. His most recent book, Tax Justice, was published by the University Press of America in 1985.

Richard Penaskovic chairs the Department of Religion at Auburn University in Alabama. He has a Ph.D. in theology from the Ludwig Maximilians University of Munich. His articles have appeared in such journals as *Augustinian Studies*, *Louvain Studies*, and *The Heythrop Journal*.

Leland J. White has his Ph.D. in theology from Duke University. He is editor of the *Biblical Theology Bulletin* and author of *Christ and the Christian Movement*, Alba House, 1985. He is an associate professor of theology at St. John's University, New York.

Foreword

THE RELATIONSHIP BETWEEN theology and authority is a perennial question. As long as there exists the discipline called theology the question of authority will always arise. Theology is the study of God. If one believes that God has revealed God's self to human beings, then the question of authority becomes important.

Christian theology attributes a special authority to the revelation of God as found in the scriptures—both the Hebrew scripture and the Christian scripture. The authority of the scripture has been discussed and debated in every century of the Christian tradition. Today in United States Protestantism the major division seems to be between those who insist that the Bible is without error—historical, scientific or otherwise, and hence immune by default to critical examination— and those who contend that the tools of historical, literary, and sociological criticism are necessary for interpreting and understanding correctly the biblical message. These different understandings of the authority of the Bible explain the difference between the fundamentalist or conservative Protestant denominations and mainline Protestants, but such divisions also exist within individual denominations such as the Southern Baptists and even the Lutherans.

The most distinctive aspect about authority in the Roman Catholic tradition is the authoritative hierarchical teaching office committed to the pope and the bishops. Roman Catholicism recognizes such a pastoral teaching office committed to pope and bishops and at the same time has traditionally given a very important role to theology and to theologians. Contemporary events as well as history have testified to the tensions and problems in the relationship between the pastoral hierarchical teaching authority and the role of theologians. The pastoral teaching function in the church has the mission of handing down the apostolic faith in the church and of teaching in matters of faith and morals. The community of theologians, on the basis of their faithful scholarship, tries to understand and appropriate the word and work of Jesus in a systematic, scientific, and reflexive manner in the light of the historical, cultural, and sociological circumstances of the present day.

To understand properly both the role of the pastoral teaching office and of the theologian in the Roman Catholic Church it becomes necessary to realize that the total church is called to creative fidelity to the word and work of Jesus. The gospel and the message of Jesus must be faithfully transmitted to the present generation. However, the Catholic tradition and self-understanding call for creative fidelity in passing on the gospel. It is not enough just to repeat what has been said in the past, but the word and work of Jesus must be understood and appropriated in the light of the contemporary circumstances of time, place, and culture. At the same time, however, it is the apostolic tradition and not something else that must be handed down.

The fourth, fifth, and sixth centuries well illustrated the meaning of creative fidelity to the gospel. At that time the early councils of the church considered the basic and core Christian teachings and taught that there are three persons in God and two natures in Jesus. Some people objected that such concepts and words came not from the scripture but from Greek philosophy. However, the total church recognized that the Christian faith had to be understood and appropriated in the light of contemporary circumstances and self-understandings.

One of the greatest theologians in the Catholic tradition is Thomas Aquinas (d. 1274). Aquinas was not content with merely repeating what those before him had said. He used the Aristotelian thought then coming into the university world of Europe to understand better the Christian faith. Aquinas employed the thought of a person who never knew Jesus and who probably did not believe in God as a means of coming to a better understanding of the Christian faith.

I am writing from the perspective of a Roman Catholic theologian. I recognize the role of and the need for the pastoral hierarchical teaching office in the church. Also, a Roman Catholic theologian must theologize within the parameters of Catholic faith. One cannot deny, for example, the role of the Petrine office in the church and still be a Roman Catholic theologian.

In the life of the church there will always be a tension between the role of theologians and the role of the hierarchical teaching office. Without such tension the church would be dead. The theologian will probe, test, and take some risks. In the process, theologians will make mistakes, but the whole church cannot be true to its function of creative fidelity to the word and work of Jesus without the function of theologians despite the inevitable mistakes that will occur.

At the present time in the Roman Catholic Church the tension between the hierarchical magisterium and theologians seems to be exaggerated and more destructive than constructive. My perspective is colored by my own experiences, but in my fallible judgment the exaggerated tensions arise from the particular historical situation in which the Roman Catholic Church finds itself today. There can be no doubt that the Second Vatican Council in the early 1960s involved a profound shift in Catholic self-understanding and life. The Catholic Church in the middle of the twentieth century was probably more authoritarian than it had been at any time in its long history. Ever since the sixteenth century Roman Catholicism adopted a negative and polemical attitude vis-à-vis Protestant Christians. Later the Catholic Church became very defensive against and suspicious of the philosophical, political, and scientific thinking of the Enlightenment and of modernity. The condemnations of Americanism, modernism, the incipient biblical renewal, and the *nouvelle théologie* in the course of the twentieth century all exemplify this overly authoritarian approach.

However, Vatican II adopted a different perspective. Dialogue with Christians and other religions as well as dialogue with the world replaced the older condemnations. The church now sees itself primarily as the people of God and as a community served by a hierarchical structure rather than a pyramid with primary importance given to the hierarchical structure at the top of the pyramid. Vatican II renewed the church, by appealing both to the signs of the times and to the older and more traditional understandings to modify the overly authoritarian self-understanding and practice of the church in the mid-twentieth century.

At the present time exaggerated tensions exist between the hierarchical teaching office and theologians precisely because the hierarchical teaching office both in theory and in practice has not sufficiently attended to the changes that occurred at the Second Vatican Council. Four areas in particular come to the fore—authority in the service of the word of God and the truth, the hierarchy of truths, ecclesiological aspects, and historical consciousness. Each of these areas will briefly be mentioned.

First, the Constitution on Divine Revelation of Vatican Council II reminds all that "the magisterium is not superior to the word of God but is its servant" (n. 10). In other words the magisterium is not above the word of God, but must itself conform to the word of God. The word of God and truth are the primary determining factors.

In the area of morality the Catholic tradition to its great credit has insisted on two important characteristics. The Catholic moral teaching on particular issues such as peace and sexuality was based on the natural law and consequently claimed to be supported by human reason. In addition, the Catholic tradition insisted that morality is intrinsic; i.e., something is commanded because it is good and not the other way around. Thus authority cannot make something right or wrong but must conform itself to the word of God and to truth.

Elemental logic recognizes that in the midst of complexity and specificity it is difficult to claim a certitude that excludes the possibility of error. All can agree that murder is always wrong, but in some specific cases it will be difficult to determine if a killing is truly a murder. The Christian person must always be just, but what is just in a complex situation might be legitimately debated among people of good will. If one accepts the rational aspect of a moral teaching, one has to acknowledge that in the midst of complexity and specificity one cannot claim to have a certitude that excludes the possibility of error. The United States bishops in their recent pastoral letters on peace and the economy have recognized that Catholics can disagree on complex questions, such as no first use of limited nuclear weapons. In these matters church authority cannot claim a degree of certainty that goes against the basic rules of rational discourse and logic. In its self-understanding and in its practical functioning the hierarchical magisterium must recognize that it is subordinate to the word of God and truth.

Second, Vatican Council II emphasized the hierarchy of truths existing within the faith. Not all the truths of faith are of the same importance. In addition there are some teachings of the church which are core and basic while others are more remote and peripheral. Ever since the late-nineteenth century Catholic teaching and church law have recognized the difference between infallible and noninfallible teaching. The official teaching maintained that Catholics must give to infallible teaching an assent of faith which is certain and absolute. However, all recognize that infallible teaching can be developed, deepened, and improved. Some critics of infallibility go much further. According to the accepted understanding, a religious respect of intellect and will is due to noninfallible teaching, and such an assent is relative and conditional. Such teaching can possibly be wrong.

In 1968 the American Catholic bishops recognized the legitimacy of public theological dissent from noninfallible teaching if the reasons are serious and well-founded, if the manner of the dissent does not question or impugn the teaching authority of the church, and if it would not cause scandal. Some people in authority in the Catholic Church today, however, do not seem to be willing to recognize the legitimacy of such theological dissent. There is general agreement within the Catholic community that even in the core beliefs of faith and in the matters that have been infallibly defined, there remains the need for a continual probing and interpretation, which should result in the deeper and better understanding of these truths. In those teachings which are more remote from the core and are noninfallible, the theological function of interpretation at times will and should take the form of dissent from the existing teachings.

Contemporary ecclesiology is a third area which has given a more nuanced view to the function of the pastoral hierarchical teaching office in the church. Without in any way denying such a hierarchical teaching function, the ecclesiology of Vatican II recognizes that such an office does not exhaust the total teaching of the church. The Constitution on the Church (n. 12), for example, recognizes the prophetic role and function existing in the church as distinguished from the hierarchical teaching office. Through baptism all Christians share in the threefold function of Jesus as priest, teacher, and sovereign. Just as the priesthood of all believers exists together with a hierarchical priesthood, so too the teaching role of all believers exists together with the hierarchical teaching office.

Historical and theological studies have also underscored the role of consultation by the faithful and reception by the faithful in determining the teaching of the church. Some theologians have talked about the existence of multiple magisteria in the church. The important point to recognize is that the total teaching role of the church cannot be reduced only to the hierarchical teaching function in the church. Such a theoretical understanding has significant practical ramifications on how the hierarchical magisterium carries out its function. Notice, for example, how the broad and public consultations employed by the United States Catholic bishops in their two recent pastoral letters on peace and the economy contrast with the way in which Roman documents are written and composed. There are many ramifications which come from the recognition that the total teaching function of the church is not identical with the hierarchical teaching function.

Fourth, one of the most significant changes associated with Vatican II is the recognition of historical consciousness. Historical consciousness is contrasted with classicism, which stresses the eternal, the universal, and the unchanging. Without falling into the opposite extreme of sheer existentialism, historical consciousness gives more importance to the particular, the individual, the contingent, and the historical.

At the very minimum historical consciousness recognizes the great diversity that has existed in history and the way in which the hierarchical teaching office has functioned. The model of the pre–Vatican II period is by no means the model that has always existed and that should always exist. History reminds us that the very term magisterium referred at one time primarily to the role of theologians and not to that of the hierarchical pastoral office. In some ecumenical councils theologians even had a vote.

Catholic thinking and teaching before Vatican II often talked about the perennial philosophy or theology which was the neoscholastic approach of the time. Historical consciousness reminds us there can be no perennial philosophy or theology. The experience of the post–Vatican II church indicates a theological pluralism existing within the church. Unfortunately, Roman teaching documents often act as if there still continues to exist within the church today a perennial philosophy or theology, and these documents cannot appreciate the legitimate pluralism rightfully existing within Catholic theology.

Both historical consciousness and ecclesiological emphasis on the collegiality of bishops call for a much greater role to be given to the national and regional conferences of bishops. However, these incipient structures are very minimal and need to be enhanced and developed. In this way the danger of an overcentralization can be overcome. Many of the frictions between theologians and the hierarchical teaching office should be dealt with on a more local level. However, here too there is need to make sure that the rights of all are duly protected.

In summary, there will always be tension between the theological role and the hierarchical teaching function in the Catholic Church. In these few lines, I have tried to indicate my judgment that the exaggerated and somewhat destructive tensions existing at the present time derive from the fact that the hierarchical teaching office in theory and in practice has not appropriated some of the changed understandings that have occurred in the Catholic Church in the light of the Second Vatican Council. However, as a Roman Catholic theologian I recognize that theologians will make mistakes and that there is always the need for a pastoral hierarchical teaching office in the church.

The perennial topic of theology and authority is even more acute today in Roman Catholicism. My primary purpose in this short essay is to introduce this volume with its many significant contributions to the problem of authority and theology. In the process of writing this foreword, I could not avoid the temptation to explain very briefly my own approach to the question. However, all of us can be enlightened and helped by the contributions in this volume which shed more light on this important issue which has so many theoretical and practical ramifications.

Charles E. Curran
Professor of Moral Theology
The Catholic University of America

Acknowledgements

To write a book is to engage in a collaborative effort with a number of colleagues. In the case of this volume the contributors make the book, and my dealings with them have been warm and gracious. I must single out Jim Dawsey for helping me proofread the galleys.

My loving wife, Nancy, has been supportive of this project from its inception. I am impressed with the efficiency and professionalism of Patrick Alexander, the editor from Hendrickson Publishers, who first approached me about publishing this book. My biggest debt of gratitude belongs to my secretary, Elsie Reynolds, who has typed the manuscript and without whose help this book would not be published.

Introduction: Every Context Includes a Context

In the church authority rules; in science and research-arguments.
Put these two together and you have problems.
Max Seckler (1978)

Theology is in its whole course at best Prologomenon,
preface. Theology speaks the preamble for that which
ultimately God himself must say.
Karl Barth (1962)

ACCORDING TO THE INFLUENTIAL JOURNAL, *The Christian Century*, the attempt of Pope John Paul II to reinstall doctrinal discipline in the Roman Catholic Church was the top religion news story of 1986. Four criteria were used by the editors of the *Century* in selecting this as the top news story: (1) the extent of media coverage; (2) the impact on religious institutions and society; (3) the historical significance and long-range implications; and (4) the moral issues involved.

The effort of the Vatican to restore doctrinal discipline directly affected Catholics in several ways. One of the top Catholic moral theologians, Professor Charles Curran, who wrote the Foreword to this book, was stripped of his license to teach theology. In December, 1979, the canonical mission of Dr. Hans Küng, one of the leading theologians in the world, was recalled. For the past decade the Dutch theologian, Edward Schillebeeckx, has had to defend himself against charges of heresy for his views on ministry and Jesus.

The *Imprimatur* has been withdrawn from such books as Anthony Wilhelm's *Christ Among Us*; pressure has been put to remove from circulation Robert Nugent's book, *Challenge to Love: Gay and Lesbian Catholics in the Church*; and the Vatican has demanded the ouster from their communities of twenty-four religious women who endorsed a statement in *The New York Times* on 7 October 1984, affirming a plurality of views on how Roman Catholics approach the abortion issue.

The credibility of the church has been exposed in these and numerous other cases because essential elements of due process were oftentimes lacking. As a result of these tactics by the Vatican, such as the removal of Archbishop Hunthausen of Seattle, Washington, from some of his main functions in his own archdiocese, the polarization between conservatives and liberals in the church has increased rather than decreased. One may see this exemplified in the violence surrounding the visit of Pope John II to the Netherlands in which protesters threw rocks and bottles at the Pope's car.

Ecumenical Input

The relationship between theology and authority is problematical not only for the Roman Catholic Church but for other churches as well. Professor John Hick, head of the Department of Religion at the Claremont Graduate School, is seeking admission as a minister to the San Gabriel Presbytery, which is part of the Presbyterian Church, U.S.A. Those who oppose his admission as a minister argue that he denies the divinity of Christ, one of the central dogmas in Christianity.

A similar controversy rages in the Mormon Church. Stan Larson in a forty-one page treatise on the *Book of Mormon*, concludes that it was not composed around A.D. 400 as contended by Joseph Smith, the founder of Mormonism in 1830. Controversy also surrounds the historians Linda King Newell and Valeen Tippetts Avery for their book, *Mormon Enigma: Emma Hale Smith*. This book concerns Joseph Smith's first wife, Emma, who strongly objected to her husband's polygamy.

The following essays deal with the topic "Theology and Authority" mainly but not exclusively in the Roman Catholic Church in hopes of shedding light on the topic for all churches. Today no church operates in a vacuum. What happens in one particular church has an impact on other churches directly as a result of the ecumenical movement. For example, the 518 member convention of the Episcopal diocese of New York unanimously resolved on 21 October 1986 to affirm full freedom in biblical and theological scholarship deploring action that constricts the area of free debate.

Granted the resolution does not specifically refer to the Roman Catholic Church. However, the Reverend Christopher Webber, who proposed the document, did so as a personal reaction to Rome's disciplinary actions against Professor Charles Curran and Raymond Hunthausen, archbishop of Seattle. The Episcopal bishop of New York, the influential Paul Moore, stated that the resolution does not point fingers, but in a world that is increasingly losing its freedom, the church ought to be a beacon of freedom rather than a sign of the impingement of it. The resolution asks for the use of authority based not on coercive discipline, but on loving witness.

It may be the case that the tension between theology and authority will never be resolved. As the quote from Max Seckler indicates, authority rules in the church, whereas in the science of theology and in theological research, arguments hold sway. Perhaps the following volume should be understood as a *Prologomenon*, a preface to what God must say.

Part 1 of these essays deals with the relationship between theology and authority mainly from the biblical and historical perspectives. The essays in Part 2 explore the question from an anthropological and/or theological point of view.

In the first essay, "Authority: The New Testament and First-Century Judaism in Cultural Perspective," David Bossman shows how in first-century Judaism, religious authority followed institutional lines and family customs in contradistinction to the Roman practice of identifying religion with the political order. He demonstrates how Jesus, who lacked both family and office, could only gain credibility by being invested with scriptural authority.

James Dawsey takes a fresh look at authority in Mark 1:22 in his essay, "Jesus and the Language of Authority." Instead of regarding the teaching of Jesus as an inert body of knowledge passed on from one generation to another, Dawsey feels we must surrender our static view of revelation which locks Jesus and his teaching into the past. Our task, then, is to opt for a dynamic view of revelation which allows God to act toward us in a new way today.

St. Francis of Assisi generally avoids using the word "authority," since it conjures up the idea of power, suggests Wayne Hellmann in "Power or Powerlessness: The Vision of Francis of Assisi." St. Francis does speak often of obedience. The role of superiors in the Franciscan fraternity consists simply in facilitating gospel obedience. The power experienced in obedience cannot be the power of one will dominating the will of another. Rather, it is the power of love or the power of powerlessness.

In her essay, "Re-thinking Authority: Imaginative Options and the Modernist Controversy," Jo Ann Eigelsbach examines the issue of authority in Wilfrid Philip Ward, a key English Roman Catholic writer at the turn of the century. Today a central question in regard to authority is this: What strategy should scholars pursue in a time of repression? W. Ward would argue that authority may only be opposed by solid research. Ward maintained that the gradual accumulation of the work of many scholars forms a weight of opinion constituting a "public authority" in the church.

An uneasy tension presently exists between the institutional and the charismatic offices in the Roman Catholic Church. In his essay, "The Contemporary Theologian: Teacher, Prophet, Doctor," Brennan Hill examines the history and nature of the charismatic teaching authority in both the early and medieval church. Dr. Hill sees the contemporary theologian exercising the charism of teaching, which exists as a gifted ministry; it nourishes the faith and thus contributes to the development of the Christian tradition. He believes that both theologians and the members of the hierarchy are servants subject to the authority of God's word and that of the Holy Spirit.

In the first essay of Part 2, "Theology and Authority: A Cross-Cultural Analysis of Theological Scripts," Leland White makes a case for understanding the expressions "theology" and "authority" historically and anthropologically. He compares cultures in terms of two variables, "group" and "grid," thus building on the work of anthropologist Mary Douglas. Finally, Professor White draws out the implications of Douglas's model for the light it sheds on the topic of theology and authority.

Ronald Pasquariello examines the notion of hierarchy as an ideology or a thought construct that legitimates the action occurring within a specific culture, namely, the Roman Catholic Church. In the current debate between conservatives and liberals in the Catholic Church, there are ideological elements, which are the root-cause of the conflict and tension. Pasquariello suggests that the ideological aspects of the present controversy over theology and authority need to be identified and avoided if there is to be any hope of breaking the impasse.

James L. Heft in "Episcopal Teaching Authority on Matters of War and Economics," asks what kind of teaching authority may the bishops of the United States exercise in regard to moral questions dealing with war and economics. Heft concludes that episcopal conferences do have a mandate to teach situated somewhere between that exercised by the individual bishop in his own diocese and that possessed by the pope and bishops gathered together in a council. Finally, in the intersection between the hierarchy and the laity, Dr. Heft sees operative a more important role for the laity in the church and a deeper appreciation of the value of noninfallible teaching authority. Of course, some of these changing roles cause a good deal of confusion in the church.

Michael Barnes, making judicious use of James Fowler's analysis of the stages of faith development, makes the point that each of these stages of development might produce a distinctive kind of theologizing. Barnes sees the appearance of stage-consciousness differences in the conflict between Hans Küng and the Vatican. Küng argues as a stage-4 or -5 consciousness might, whereas the Vatican usually restricts itself to styles most consistent with stage 3. Since both sides operate on different stages of faith development, mutual understanding becomes exceedingly difficult.

The final essay, "Theology and Authority: The Theological Issues," puts the blame for the strained relationship between the magisterium (or teaching authority of the church) and theologians on two competing views of the church, the institutional model of the church over against the church understood as the people of God. Another source of tension between the magisterium and theologians stems from the fact that Rome today still thinks of Catholic theology in terms of ahistorical scholasticism as opposed to a more historically conscious theology. The essay concludes with some suggestions for a renewed magisterium in the church.

R.P.

Part 1

Part 1

Authority: The New Testament and First-Century Judaism in Cultural Perspective

David Bossman

Department of Religious Studies
Seton Hall University

W HEN VIEWED WITHIN THE SOCIAL WORLD of first-century Mediterranean culture, questions dealing with the character and function of authority in the New Testament and first-century Judaism raise several key issues:[1] (1) the setting and function of religion in the New Testament world; (2) the character of institutional authority in first-century Judaism; (3) the nature of Jesus' authority and leadership; and (4) the developments within communities which nurtured Christian beliefs and practice.

By centering discussion on these areas of cross-cultural examination, the nature and function of authority in the New Testament and first-century Judaism can emerge more authentically within its native setting.[2] Given the necessity and value of viewing the New Testament world across cultural lines (ours and theirs), it will be worthwhile to investigate first the ways in which religious authority functioned in the New Testament world before any legitimate implications of that authority can be drawn for application outside of the biblical environment, in our own time and culture.

I. Religion in the New Testament World

Present-day North Americans often see the church as the independent, institutional setting or context for the functioning of religion, where separate church laws apply and religious authorities work out their respective ecclesiastical roles. This assumption is based on an historical separation of church and state that is basic to American polity. Even when viewing the church internationally, it often appears to Americans that other cultures must recognize the institutional integrity of churches as independent religious institutions.

Most North Americans would be surprised to discover that Mediterranean society in New Testament times characteristically lacked such an independent religious institution.[3] Instead, religion existed as a function of the state or within the setting of the (extended) family (e.g. religion as a function of the state of a kin-group practice).

A study of religious authority, then, must begin with an assessment of where and how religious authority functioned in the New Testament and first-century Judaism. In asking such a question of the New Testament text, we are recognizing the necessity of embarking on a cross-cultural analysis of the New Testament world, viz. by prescinding from our own cultural assumptions and practices in favor of recognizing the cultural structures and practices of a different time and place.

The manner in which various New Testament writers address their audiences suggests how religious affiliation is perceived within the community of the author. Paul, for example, recognizes a familial bond with his fellow Jews. He expresses a fraternal relationship of flesh and blood (Rom 9:3-4), referring to them as "my brothers, my kinsmen the Israelites," a mode of expression often characteristic of Paul's fellow Jews, notably the Pharisees. He describes an adopted son status for Israel (Rom 9:4) as well as for all who are led by the Spirit of God. Such people, Christians and Jews, address God as Abba, Father, (Rom 8:14-15) and are children of God (Rom 8:16-17, 19, 21). Correspondingly, Paul addresses Christians as "brothers" and "sisters" (Rom 14:10, 13, 15, 21; 16:1, 1 Cor 1:1; 5:11; 7:12, 15; 9:5; etc.). Using such terms symbolically, Paul indicates that in his view Judaism, and in like manner Christianity, is likened to an extended family or kinship group in which the religion of the father is continued through "adoption" and blood-line procreation. Specifically, the fictive kinship or extended family religion manifests the characteristics of familial or kinship relationships, calling for familylike affiliation and loyalty.

In first-century Judaism, the accepted practice of maintaining religion within the family and utilizing familial symbolism continued and was associated with other family practices and kinship obligations.[4] One such concurrence of religious and family custom was in the area of marriage. Since marriages were viewed as strategic covenants,[5] and procreation was seen to have effects in the continuity of both family and religion, marriage was carefully controlled by the custom of endogamy (marriage within a specific tribe or similar social unit), and the practice of marrying within the clan was carefully observed whenever possible. Monogamy developed within a context of defensive strategies for Jewish family continuity, to assure the maintenance of the family line as well as to safeguard the family's religious customs.[6] Monogamous family procreation, "godly offspring" (Mal 3:15), reminiscent of Ezra's notion of the holy offspring (Ezra 9:2), was seen as proper religious observance as well as an assurance of continuity in the Jewish family line.[7]

The purity code, derived substantially from the priestly tradition, formulated social lines and practices which clearly set the boundaries between "us" (Jews) and "them" (non-Jews).[8] This basic social exclusiveness is both familial and religious in its application and expectations for all members of the kinship group.

The defensive marriage strategy also extended into the manner and motivation of parents' choosing marriage partners for their children. Since holy offspring were the explicit purpose of marital unions (Mal 2:15), and this was a religious norm hosted in the family institution, then marriage for wealth or other purposes (e.g. sexual attractiveness) was shameful and immoral (Tobit 6:16, 18; 8:7, 10).

Religious authority among significant groups in first-century Judaism tended to follow institutional lines and customs of family and kinship structures.[9] This was in contrast with the Roman practice of identifying religion with the political order. Thus, for Romans, not only was the practice of religion a state function, but also the role of the emperor had a distinctively religious character, so that religion and politics became indistinguishable in symbolism and ritual. Political loyalty was expressed in religious observances.

The association of religion with the state was characteristic of Judaism during some periods of history and continued among notable factions within Judaism into and beyond the New Testament period.[10] In these more aggressive periods, marriage strategies (the process of choosing wives or husbands for political advantage among families), likewise followed an aggressive pattern of alliance building and were utilized for economic as well as political ends. Such was the case during the Solomonic period when temple and cult were under royal sponsorship, and marriage covenants joined international royal families for mutual benefit. Such alliance building and familiarity with foreigners was the object of deuteronomic scorn (1 Kgs 11:1-11; Deut 7:3-4; 17:15-17). We can observe in the pro-and anti-monarchy polemics of 1 Samuel 8-11 a tension between the proper placement of religion in the traditional family/clan setting and the proper function of a divinely sanctioned political order.

In the post-exilic period, the priestly aristocracy allied with the political functionaries to form pacts of mutual support either under the title of temple maintenance or in pursuit of a Jewish religious state. It was such a state of affairs that underscored the conflicts between Sadducees and Pharisees during the reigns of Alexander Janaeus and his successor Alexandra Salome.[11] Characteristically, the Sadducees maintained alliances with the political potentates, and the Pharisees held to traditional family mores and household observance of Judaism. By contrast, the Essenes tended to reject the political alliances of the Jerusalem aristocracy with Rome in favor of pursuing an alternative political identity in a Jewish religious state under the leadership of a political messianic figure whose righteous religious credentials matched his political power.

The debate continued throughout the New Testament period in the grievance of the Pharisees with the accommodations of the more politically inclined Sadducees and with the Jerusalem priesthood, which was willing to accept state support for the temple and thereby acknowledge the power of the foreign state in subsuming religion. For the Pharisees, the politicization of religion involved wrenching religion from its proper family setting, hence, it meant compromising the expressions of religious observance within the structures of the extended family (not as in the modern nuclear family but in the broader sense of family which was inclusive of the household, clan, and tribe rather than the individual husband-wife-children family unit). For the Essenes, politicization was not the problem; it was embedding religion in the wrong state, in the Roman instead of the Jewish state, hence the accommodating Jerusalemite priesthood had in the Essene ideology misplaced their loyalty in Rome rather than in God.[12]

Jewish customs predominate in religious discussions of this period and are often placed in contrast to requirements of Roman law (John 19:7; Acts 18:15). For Pharisees, the "oral law" (really customs rather than legislation) was the means by which the vitality of biblical norms could be maintained. This follows the family model of traditions of particular observance (customs) as opposed to the more standardized application of laws by the state in juridical fashion. Jewish customs view various rabbinic interpretations as diverse patriarchal-like applications of norms for particular disciple/family groups. Among the Pharisees, the family model of custom was the principle legal context for religious observance, e.g. maintaining separation from non-Jews, observing endogamous marriage restrictions, rendering due respect to parental authority, recognizing the mutual obligations of Jews to one another as members of one family (e.g. Tobit 4:12-13; Jub 20:3; 4 Macc 5:16-25). Such customs were maintained by the process of reciprocity within the extended family environment of Pharisaic Judaism.

Within first-century Judaism, thus, there remained the age-old question, in which institutional setting should religion reside, in the family or in the state? The Pharisees and perhaps the majority of ordinary Jews who retained the family setting as the most hospitable milieu of religious observance, saw in the household of Judaism the safest and most effective context for the practice and transmission of Judaism. The Sadducees, Jerusalem priests, Essenes, and Zealots saw religion in the realm of politics, each in its own light. The question remained open as the New Testament writers chose where to situate their individual community's view as they came to formulate portraits of Jesus and his role in emerging Christianity.

II. Jesus and Leadership

Within the setting of first-century Judaism, Jesus' leadership was conspicuously lacking in foundation, that is to say, his family was not influential in Jewish or Roman society, and he held no office other than those ascribed to him as subsequently interpretive of the manner of his fulfilling needs and traditional expectations. Simply put, Jesus is presented as a preacher of religious observance in his day, and at the same time he is characterized as an upholder and interpreter of the law (Mark 1:44; 10:3; Matt 5:17-18; 7:12; Luke 16:17; John 5:45-46).

Given Jesus' lack of a legitimate basis for institutional authority, political or familial, one wonders how the New Testament writers could infer authority within a society already structured in matters religious according to kinship norms and political affiliations. By which authority model does Jesus bind people to standards or norms if, in fact, he does exercise authority and call for the observance of new or particular standards or norms?

The first title suggesting Jesus' authority base in sonship. Although Jesus is only secondarily linked with Joseph, Matthew and Luke both trace his lineage through Joseph, taking different paths to his family ties with famous biblical personages (Luke through David to Abraham and ultimately to Adam; Matthew through David to Abraham). The theme of Jesus' sonship in the Davidic line occurs principally in the Infancy Narratives as the purpose for his being born in Bethlehem (suggesting a royal messianic role) and as such is regarded as a secondary level of treatment. This identification of Jesus as the son of David seems, as interpreted by Vermes, to be separable from the honorific greeting in Mark 10:47-48 and parallels (Luke 18:38-39; Matt 20:30-31, as well as in 9:27), yet as a son of David, Jesus is filling a political role and the messianic theme here follows a royal identification which more readily relates to the divinely constituted state than with the family.

Elsewhere in the New Testament, Paul describes Jesus as "descended from David according to the flesh" (Rom 1:3), a lineage repeated in 2 Tim 2:8. It seems that such references to the Davidic title and lineage, following Vermes, do not provide enough of a basis for drawing historical conclusions about Jesus' actual descent. They do, however, affirm a political messianic theme which has been applied to Jesus at some stage in the tradition.

References to Jesus' being son of God are more frequent throughout the New Testament. By this designation, Jesus is recognized as holding a position of election (Mark 1:11; 9:7; Matt 3:17; 17:5) and in a relationship of familiarity with God (Matt 11:27; Mark 12:6; John 3:35) whom he addresses as Father (Matt 11:25-27; Mark 14:36; Luke 10:21-22; John 12:28). Jesus is portrayed as assuming the title with reference to himself in two texts: Mark 13:32 (Matt 24:36) and Matt 11:27 (Luke 10:22). In both instances there is reason to argue for a later inclusion of the title "son of God" and to doubt Jesus' own use of the title with reference to himself.[13] Other designations used descriptively or in address also are likely enough later accretions to the gospel tradition or are used as broad rather than literal descriptives.

The possession of power, as for instance in the temptations, where Satan links sonship of God with the ability to command service, seems clearly not to be a function of Jesus' relationship to God as son. Jesus demurs in favor of a more dutiful expression of sonship: "'If you are the Son of God, command these stones to turn into bread.' Jesus replied, 'Scripture has it: "Not on bread alone is man to live but on every utterance that comes from the mouth of God"'" (Matt 4:3-4).

The title, Son of Man, is more linked with power, suggesting that the eschatological title is indicative of the actual exercise of authority.

This is especially striking in the change of titles in Matt 26:63 where the high priest asks Jesus whether or not he is "the Messiah, the Son of God." Jesus' words change title and make reference to the eschatological role of the Son of Man: "It is you who say it. But I tell you this: Soon you will see the Son of Man seated at the right hand of the Power and coming on the clouds of heaven" (26:64). Elsewhere the title Son of Man is likewise linked with power (Matt 9:6; 24:30; Mark 2:10), and associated with the kingship and kingdom (Mark 8:38-9:1; Matt 13:41; 16:28). In transmitting power and authority to his disciples, Jesus manifests his kingship and kingdom as expressions of the exercise of power and its conferral (Matt 16:19), with clear allusion to the messianic character of the power.

In these titles of Jesus we see dimensions of personal authority, which are derived from Jesus' relation of sonship, with political undertones and ramifications. Curiously, Jesus himself seems to eschew the political dimension of his authority and power as he characteristically forewarns all who witness it to keep it secret (Matt 16:20, etc.). Consequently, there never seems to be clarity about what authority Jesus actually claimed for himself or what is most appropriate in describing him. His authority seems to be likened to the authority in the titles which are applied to him in virtually midrashic fashion, by finding traditional biblical themes which somehow can be drawn upon to aptly characterize him. Thus, Jesus' authority is not drawn from the various quasi-offices brought forward from the biblical tradition to sketch a biblical likeness of the movement's hero. Rather, Jesus is viewed as having authority which is similar to the titles ascribed to him in a midrashic mode. The writers have examined the scriptures in hopes of finding the appropriate language to describe the phenomenon experienced in the person of Jesus.

This then leads to another kind of personal authority which can aptly describe in nonbiblical terms what the New Testament writers used traditional biblical terms to depict in midrashic fashion. This kind of personal authority Malina calls *reputational* authority, and it "is rooted in a person's ability to influence a change in the broadly encompassing norms that constrain recognition of legitimate authority."[14] Reputational authority accords well with the "partly the same and partly different" character of the titles which the evangelists apply to Jesus. It is not to deny the value of the similitudes, but rather to coalesce their categories in order to find a fundamental concept that more adequately encapsulates the encoded message of the evangelists for modern readers.

In this role of reputational authority, Jesus effectively calls into question the religious messages of those who smotheringly claim legitimate authority, and by ventilating their categories he convinces his hearers that the exercise of their authority can rightly be called into question. In a word, reputational authority is based upon the ability of a person to persuade effectively others, to convince them of a deeper truth or higher standard, which the recognized authority is violating in the exercise of otherwise legitimate authority.

Reputational authority, Malina observes, emerges within societies in which there is a pervading doubt about the effectiveness of a social system in achieving the values to which the society aspires. This seems clearly to be the case in first-century Judaism in which there is social alienation from both the political leaders who have ineffectively subsumed the religious system as well as against the leaders of family-based religion. Jesus scores both alike:

> "Be on your lookout against the yeast of the Pharisees and Sadducees. . . ."
> They finally realized that he was not issuing a warning against yeast but against the Pharisees' and Sadducees' teaching (Matt 16:6, 12).

So also:

> Woe to you Pharisees! You pay tithes on mind and rue and all the garden plants, while neglecting justice and the love of God. These are the things you should practice, without omitting the others (Luke 11:42).

The question which may be raised, then, centers on the effect of Jesus' reputational authority. If the person with reputational authority succeeds in convincing others, then a vacuum occurs, "deregulating" customs espoused by the previous authorities and calling for norms to be brought forward to re-regulate, i.e. to reintegrate the society's standards into an institutional form. Hence, while the Gospels portray Jesus in a manner which can be taken as founded in kinship (Son of God) and the realm of politics (Son of Man, Messiah), his true identity is really neither but rather a call for the reexamination of both.

Jesus showed scant inclination and took virtually no steps toward institutionalizing religion in himself or in any particular new form. If anything, it is the ordinariness of Jesus with regard to offices of state or family name recognition which makes him stand out. He personally seems never to aspire to do or be more than one who exposes the barrenness of would-be authorities in favor of a more foundational principal for thinking or acting. What transformed him into a leader of a religious movement was the need and impetus of his followers who championed in him what he himself never seemed to claim, a form of political leader whose titles derived from ancient national glories and aspirations.

In Jesus, his followers could convincingly argue for the restoration of messianic kingship and the establishment of the kingdom with its eschatological lord. He had the potential to reintegrate all of Israel's fallow aspirations without the need to find paths to their realization other than in recognition of the simple fact of the unavailability of alternatives. It was on this point that fellow Jews could be rendered vulnerable by the enthusiasm of Jesus' followers (Mark 11:18; 12:12). Because of claims to a reintegration of Israel's political/religious coalition, another and more powerful claimant might step in to thwart the perceived threat and nip it in the bud. Such was the case as Jesus entered Jerusalem at one particularly volatile Passover (Mark 14:61-63; John 19:15), and continued through the formative period of Christianity's development (Acts 16:20-24; 17:6-7).

III. Developments in the Communities which Nurtured Christian Beliefs

There is little doubt today that the New Testament writers portrayed Jesus in ways that responded to their needs and interpretations rather than to set out a simple history of the man in his own time and place. This is less reprehensible to the modern reader than an expected reflection of the fact that Jesus' impact transcended his execution, as the Gospels clearly propound (Matt 28:16-20; Mark 16:15-18; Luke 24:25-35; John 16:7, 16, 26-27); and his resurrection was partly at least manifested in the continuation of his teaching in the newly created families that espoused him as the ground for their adoption by the Father (Rom 8:15, 21; Gal 4:5) and incorporation into the body of his faithful (John 15:4; Eph 1:23).

The continuing influence of his teaching and the manifestation of his presence within the early Christian communities bears witness to a manifestation of authority implicit in his life and teaching but expressed in early households of faith. These house-church communities of early Christianity formed the matrix for the development of Christian values and aspirations. They were not the large ecclesial dioceses of later times, and if they are mistakenly viewed in that way their witnesses lose much of their authenticity and meaning. Rather, the early Christian communities were fictive families or household-churches which related one with the other as families characteristically do, with vaguely common purposes but also with occasional tensions and conflicts.[15] If one were to look for organizational structure it would be a vain search, for little is suggested in the teaching of Jesus and little is expected in the family setting.

Paul's writings paint portraits of troubled Christian communities as households in a state of constant conflict and feuding rather than in quiet expectation and peaceful piety. In his irenic analogy of the Christian community as a body (1 Cor 12:12), each person having assigned roles and functions, Paul only underscores the lack of such harmony and the need for a more reflective response to the teaching of Jesus (1 Cor 12:27-31; 3:1-4; Gal 3:1). Moreover, such households of the faith admitted of great variation in their adaptive responses to the environmental factors which brought pressures to bear on their familial group, as each of the gospel communities clearly exemplified in their presentation of Jesus through the lenses of their evangelist-redactor.

Most notably lacking among the emerging Christian house-churches in the Roman Empire was what other religions regarded as "true doctrine," which simply meant ancient tradition or customs.[16] Lacking such antiquity as followers of the Galilean rabbi, and emerging from a Jewish milieu yet not adhering to its religious customs, Christians were at a disadvantage in winning adherents from the educated classes, which quickly spotted such shortcomings. What resulted in first-century Christianity was destructive tensions with Jews and lack of understanding by Gentiles. Following Paul, what was clearly needed was documentation which would apologetically explain who Jesus was and on what basis their belief in him had the weight of ancient tradition. Lacking family and office, such a rabbi and miracle worker could only survive the tests of credibility by investing him with the authority which scripture alone could provide. Hence, Jesus was portrayed in midrashic style, affirming his relationship to the panoply of biblical personages in whose traditions he not only achieved great works but transcended all understanding. By his resultant authority, disciples carried on in his name the great works and traditions of the past, bringing to the world the vision which Jews expected as the rightful role of their messianic vindicator.

Notes

1. The author is indebted to the social science method exemplified by B. J. Malina in such works as "The Individual and the Community—Personality in the Social World of Early Christianity," *BTB* 9 (1979): 126-38; *The New Testament World: Insights from Cultural Anthropology* (Atlanta: John Knox, 1981); "The Social Sciences and Biblical Interpretation," *Int* 36 (1982): 229-42; "Jesus as Charismatic Leader," *BTB* 14 (2, 1984): 55-62; *Christian Origins and Cultural Anthropology: Practical Models for Biblical Interpretation*, (Atlanta: John Knox, 1986). This method has elsewhere been exemplified in the writings of L. J. White., "Grid and Group in Matthew's Community: The Righteousness/ Honor Code in the Sermon on the Mount," *Social-Scientific Criticism of the New Testament and Its Social World*, ed. J. H. Elliott, *Semeia* 35 (1986); L. J. White, "Mapping Economic Life in the Bible," *Pastoral Life* 35 (3, 1986): 30-38; John J. Pilch, "Leprosy and Body Symbolism," *BTB* 11 (1981): 108-13 (1981): J. H. Neyrey, "The Idea of Purity in Mark's Gospel," *Semeia* 35 (1986): 91-124; J. H. Elliott, "Social-Scientific Criticism of the New Testament: More on Methods and Models," *Semeia* 35 (1986). A similar approach, but not constructing or verifying the models as in the social-scientific method exemplified in the preceeding works is taken in the descriptive social history by Wayne Meeks, *The First Urban Christians: The Social World of the Apostle Paul* (New Haven, Conn.: Yale University Press, 1983).

2. L. J. White further demonstrates this critical method in this volume. See "Theology and Authority: A Cross-Cultural Analysis," ch. 6.

3. Two current publications underscore the importance of this cultural phenomenon and its significance for cross-cultural analysis: B. J. Malina, " 'Religion' in the World of Paul," *BTB* 16 (3, 1986): 92-101; R. L. Wilken, "Religious Pluralism and Early Christian Theology," *Int* 40 (4, 1986): 379-91. Malina more methodologically explores the subject while Wilkens recognizes its significance for an awareness of functional pluralism in the Roman Empire. He notes: "Religion was less a matter of holding beliefs than of observing annual festivals or public rituals, less concerned with conversion than adherence, of participating in local cults without, however, excluding others, of identifying with the traditions of the city in which one lived. Seldom did it require conscious choice. In the Roman Empire there was no term corresponding to our word 'religion' (i.e. a set of beliefs, a form of ritual, a code of behavior, an organization, and a common memory)" (p. 380). See also D. S. Russell, "Cultural and Religious Developments in the Hellenistic Age," in *From Early Judaism to Early Church* (Philadelphia: Fortress, 1986), 1-18.

4. See S. Safrai, "Home and Family," in *The Jewish People in the First Century*, ed. S. Safrai and M. Stern, (Philadelphia: Fortress, 1976), 2:778-92.

5. B. J. Malina, presents a detailed and valuable account of first-century Mediterranean cultural kinship and marriage practices in "Kinship and Marriage" in *The New Testament World*, 94-121.

6. See D. M. Bossman, "The Marriage Reform of Ezra: Israel Redefined," *BTB* 9 (1, 1979): 32-38.

7. For a fuller rabbinic treatment of this subject see Safrai, "Home and Family," 748-50, e.g., "The ideal of marriage was the perpetuation of the family line, and so the number and survival of children was seen as the family's chief blessing. . . . If after ten years his marriage had no issue, a man was required to divorce his wife and take another" (p. 750).

8. Consult Safrai, "Religion in Everyday Life" in *The Jewish People in the First Century*, 828-32. In listing the causes for ritual pollution, Safrai cites first those found in Torah, then those developed during the post-biblical period. Note that any form of contact with outsiders was ground for pollution, clearly a defensive ban on outside contacts: "We list here the main grounds for ritual impurity. . . . Oral law added: 'the non-Jew, his (i.e. entering the non-Jew's) main residence, land outside the Land of Israel, and idolatry' " (pp. 828-29). Safrai cites as an example of the second entering a non-Jew's residence, John 18:28: "They did not enter the praetorium (of Pilate) themselves, for they had to avoid ritual impurity if they were to eat the Passover supper. Pilate came out to them."

9. Religious rituals and observance were therefore principally found within the context of the family and in everyday home activities. See J. Neusner, "The Pharisees," in *Judaism in the Beginning of Christianity* (Philadelphia: Fortress, 1984), 45-61, esp. 58-60 where Neusner notes how women gained a specialized role in Pharisaic religion precisely because of the heightened emphasis on home observance. Safrai adds that "individuals, families or associations could apply their own measure of rigor, or stress one particular commandment, or take on works of supererogation . . . the spontaneous outcome of a religious vitality on the lookout for new ways of expressing itself" ("Religion in Everyday Life," 795). This is a further indication that religion was home-based and a function of family life among many Jews of the first century.

10. The Sadducees, for instance, in contrast to the Pharisees, in their aristocratic high priestly role often allied with the political establishment. Safrai notes: "The high priests followed the Sadducean trend, while the people tended to follow the Pharisees and became estranged from the high priesthood. The people regarded the Pharisaic doctors of the Law as their teachers, and obeyed them and stood by them in the clash between the Pharisees and the Sadducean high priesthood. . . . Even the high priests' closeness to the monarchy and their national and political position contributed to the dimming of their image and the lessening of their influence among the people" ("Jewish Self Government," *The Jewish People in the First Century*). The Pharisees allowed and encouraged variations in family activities cited in note 9 above, while the Sadducees limited the range of religious practice to a more conservative range of activities, centered around the officially recognized temple and state observances.

11. Safrai, "Jewish Self Government," 384, 388; also, S. Applebaum, "Economic Life in Palestine," *The Jewish People in the First Century*, 2, 636.

12. See, for instance, Russell, 11-12; Neusner, *Judaism in the Beginning of Christianity*, 18, 25-26. A useful anthology of texts on the various factions and groups in first-century Judaism is available in *Faith and Piety in Early Judaism: Texts and Documents*, ed. G. W. E. Nickelsburg and M. E. Stone (Philadelphia:

Fortress, 1983). See esp. 24-41 on the Pharisees, Sadducees, Essenes, and Zealots.

13. G. Vermes, *Jesus the Jew: A Historian's Reading of the Gospels* (New York: Macmillan, 1973), 156-57.

14. Malina, *Christian Origins*, 118-19.

15. W. Munro, with a critical eye to the male domination involved, surveys the Pastoral Epistles and 1 Peter with household churches emerging in high relief: *Authority in Paul and Peter: The Identification of A Pastoral Stratum in the Pauline Corpus and 1 Peter* (Cambridge: Cambridge University Press, 1983), 97-103. See also: E. Schweizer, *Church Order in the New Testament* (London: SCM, 1961), 78-79; H. von Campenhausen, *Ecclesiastical Authority and Spiritual Power* (London: A. & C. Black, 1969) 76, 107, 116 as cited by Munro. Compare Neusner in *Judaism in the Beginning of Christianity*, 58-60 on the role of women in Pharisaism.

16. R. L. Wilken, "Religious Pluralism and Early Christian Theology," 382.

Jesus and the Language of Authority

2

James Dawsey

Department of Religion
Auburn University

THERE ARE MANY PUZZLES in the Gospel of Mark. Near the beginning of the Gospel, soon after Jesus began his ministry, he went with some disciples to Capernaum. On the Sabbath, he entered the synagogue where Mark records that "they were astonished at his teaching for he taught them as one who had authority and not as the scribes" (Mark 1:22). The scene in Mark is so quickly drawn that it is not certain whether Jesus' teaching was directed to the disciples or to the crowd. Likewise, it is not immediately clear who exactly was astonished at Jesus' teaching. From the summary statement in Mark 1:28, it appears that the "all" *(hapantes)* of Mark 1:26 refers to everyone in the synagogue and not exclusively to the disciples—but as I just noted, Jesus' audience is not well defined. The evangelist sacrificed quite a number of the minor elements of his story in order to emphasize the authority *(exousia)* of Jesus' teaching.

The following essay will explore more closely this authority mentioned in Mark. What was it about Jesus' teaching that caused astonishment? In what way was his teaching powerful? How actually was Jesus' teaching different from that of the experts in the law? Although these questions have historical roots, my final purpose is not to reconstruct history, but to question the relevance of the authority of Jesus' teaching for today's Christian. In what way is Jesus' teaching authoritative for us?

I. Jesus and the Experts in the Law

There are two common interpretations for *exousia* in Mark 1:22. One locates the authority of Jesus with the manner by which he taught.[1]

His authority is said to rest in his person—rather than in his message. The point is that he spoke with power. The authority was in his delivery of the message. Whereas the scribes were merely interpreters of the law, Jesus was the Son of God who had received the Spirit at baptism and could teach with the authority of God. The scribes had derived their authority from their study and their desire to be obedient to the law. In contrast, Jesus possessed direct authority. When Jesus taught in the synagogue, his hearers sensed his charisma and knew that they were in the presence of someone special.

There is much to commend this interpretation, especially since there are several passages in the Gospel of Mark where authority does seem to be used this way—as a personal characteristic of Jesus (see Mark 2:10; 3:15; 6:7). Nevertheless, there are also some problems with this reading of Mark 1:22. Perhaps the most serious is a literary difficulty. Mark 1:22 clearly joins the amazement of those in the synagogue to the teaching itself (*exeplēssonto epi tē didachē autou*) and not to Jesus' delivery. For instance, the author of Mark could have easily written that the people in the synagogue were astonished at Jesus' power rather than at his teaching (cf. Luke 4:32, 36). This is perhaps even more evident a few verses later where the evangelist wrote that Jesus' audience asked "What thing is this? A new teaching with authority" (Mark 1:27). Had the author wanted to emphasize Jesus' personal authority, I imagine that he would have written rather, "Who is this? A new teacher with authority."

An allied difficulty concerns the lack of understanding and the growing rejection that accompanies Jesus' ministry in Mark. As is common knowledge, the author penned a secrecy motif into the Gospel showing how Jesus hid his identity from his followers who did not fully recognize him for who he was.

It is interesting to note the extent to which Jesus, in Mark, does not betray himself through his own speech. For instance, except for the highly sarcastic saying in Mark 6:4, Jesus does not admit to being a prophet. More significantly, however, Jesus does not adopt the characteristics of prophetic speech in the first half of Mark—as he does in Matthew and Luke—that would cause him to be easily identified as a prophet. The absence of *makarioi* and *plēn*, and the near absence of *ouai* in Jesus' speech in Mark provide good examples. But why would the Gospel writer have gone to so much effort to hide Jesus' language of authority in the narrative if at the same time he assumed that the authority of Jesus' person was immediately evident to anyone who heard him speak?

With the rejection of Jesus, this problem becomes more acute. If Jesus' authority was of a personal, charismatic type, why did his followers reject him? How is it possible that people who instantly recognized his authority early in the Gospel and were amazed at it, could have conspired to kill him late in the Gospel? Were they disillusioned? Did they change their mind about his authority? Probably not, because near the end of the Gospel the crowd continues to be astonished at Jesus' teaching (Mark 11:18) and the temple leaders, at least, ask him concerning his authority (Mark 11:27-33). While Jesus' teaching remains in some manner authoritative, he himself is put to death.

Urged on by some of these difficulties, David Daube suggested that *exousia* may correspond to the Hebrew *rshvth* and denote a special ordination or license superior to that conferred on elementary teachers of the law—in this case, the scribes. Jesus then, in Mark, would be a teacher who had the authority to introduce new rules.[2] But as A. W. Argyle pointed out, this is very unlikely.[3] The authority that the evangelist envisioned seems not to rest only on the person of Jesus or the delivery of his teaching.

A second common interpretation that is offered for Mark 1:22 is based on the recognition that the authority of Jesus relates more directly to his message. In Jesus' day the scribes seem to have been ordained theologians, probably Pharisees, who had special training in the written and oral law. They practiced halachah (interpretation) and were interested in the preservation of the legal system built on scripture. They seem to have been so concerned to make scripture apply to every aspect of life that they used much latitude in interpreting it and on occasion could evade its obvious sense if it caused embarrassment.

Could it be then that Jesus was different than the scribes in that he sought out the heart of the law? Whereas the scribes paid much attention to observing the superficial details of the law and ignored its essence, could it be that the people were amazed that Jesus' teaching affirmed the core of God's commandments? We could hypothesize that the people in the synagogue in Capernaum recognized in Jesus' type of teaching the authority of Jeremiah and Ezekiel who had also called attention to the essence of the law (see Jer 31:33; Ezek 36:26-28). Jesus' true interpretation is set over against the hypocrisy of the scribes.

Again, there is much to commend this interpretation of the authority of Jesus' teaching. The best support for this view, however, comes not from Mark but from Matthew.[4] The parallel to Mark 1:22 occurs at Matt 7:28-29, at the end of the Sermon on the Mount, where certainly Jesus tries to voice an essential understanding of the law. He appears as a prophet like Moses, giving many commandments. Moreover, in that sermon Jesus attacks the scribes for their casuistry, which defeats the true will of God (Matt 5:21-48).[5]

But there is little to lead us to believe that the evangelist intended in Mark 1:22 to compare Jesus' true interpretation of the law with a superficial interpretation of the scribes. I will list three reasons. First, while Jesus (and the evangelist) might have thought that the scribes were hypocrites, there is little indication that the people in the synagogue would have thought so. The only passage that might indicate that sentiment on the part of the people occurs much later at Mark 12:37. Rather, in the eyes of the people, the scribes retain their prestige throughout the Gospel. It is difficult to imagine that Jesus' audience in the synagogue would have understood the casuistry of the scribes as an indication that their teaching was inferior. To the contrary, they probably would have taken it to be a sign of the scribes' superiority.

Second, it is a scribe in the Gospel of Mark who recognizes the true essence of the law (see Mark 12:28-34). On the whole, the Markan Jesus did not think well of the scribes, but the reason seems to be more their lack of humility, selflessness, and sincerity than their teaching (see Mark 12:38-40).

And third, Jesus' only recorded teaching in Mark before Mark 1:22 does not even concern the observance of the law. Jesus' message is that "the time is fulfilled, and the kingdom of God is at hand: repent and believe the gospel" (Mark 1:15). Since no other teaching is given, we can assume that this is the teaching that astonished the people in the synagogue.[6] But this teaching does not seem to have been substantially different in its content from the teaching of the scribes. For example, the Kaddish Prayer appears to have been "Magnified and sanctified be his great name in the world which he has created according to his purpose. May he establish his kingdom in your days in your lifetime and in the lifetime of all the house of Israel, even speedily and at a near time. And say ye, Amen."[7] So, why would this teaching, which after all also follows the message of John the Baptist and Jewish apocalyptic in general, have elicited astonishment?

Perhaps we should begin by asking why the scribes have been singled out in Mark 1:22. If the author had in mind the authority of Jesus' person, why would he not have had the people in the synagogue compare

Jesus to governors or high priests, that is, to leaders with a great deal
of personal authority? But, why the scribes? Could it be that the author
of Mark wanted to compare the openness of Jesus' proclamation with
the hidden wisdom of the scribes?[8]

It has been suggested that the authority of Jesus' teaching lay in the
open form of his teaching.[9] Jesus spoke clearly. He revealed the truth.
Everything was above board with him. This perhaps makes more sense
if we keep in mind the importance of the oral law to the scribes. The
Pharisees held that Moses had passed down through seventy elders a
secret body of knowledge which was purer than the written law because
it had not been corrupted by writing. The scribes were the ones who
were trained in this special wisdom.

But the best and perhaps the only evidence for this view of Jesus'
authority comes from a difficult interpretation of a difficult passage,
Mark 4:9-23. According to Elton Trueblood's reading of this pericope,
when Jesus is alone, he is approached by some people who are seeking
some private insight into this teaching (Mark 4:10). Jesus answers with
an ironic statement, trying to point out that he intends his message to
be understood by all. His parables are not meant to hide the truth and
perpetuate sin (Mark 4:11-12). After explaining the parable (Mark
4:13-20), Jesus then reaffirms that his message is not intended to be
hidden (Mark 4:21-23).[10]

But even if we grant that this reading of Mark 4:9-23 is the correct
one, what does it say about the authority of Jesus' teaching in Mark
1:22? The scribes are not mentioned in Mark 4 and there is no real
evidence in Mark 1 that the people of the synagogue thought Jesus'
teaching "more open" than that of the scribes. Moreover, this view
misrepresents the scribes, who, after all, would have been thought of
by the people as trying to unlock the innermost meaning of scripture.

II. Jesus' New Teaching

The commonly offered explanations for the authority of Jesus' teaching
in Mark 1:22 do not fully satisfy. The authority does not seem to rest
solely on Jesus' person, or in the directness and openness of his message.

But there is one possibility that I have not yet mentioned. In an
article entitled "The Terminology of Mark's Exorcism Stories" Howard
Clark Kee suggested that the authority of Jesus is supremely manifest
in the exorcism accounts.[11] This insight might help us with *exousia* in
Mark 1:22. While in the synagogue, Jesus heals a man with an unclean

spirit (Mark 1:23-26). Then Mark reports that "they were all amazed, so that they questioned among themselves, saying, 'What is this? A new teaching with authority! He commands even the unclean spirits, and they obey him'" (Mark 1:27). Here, the people say that the teaching is new and in the same breath, link it to the exorcism. That is why Kee claims that the authority of Jesus' word and the authority of his action are united in the exorcisms.[12] But in what way is Jesus' teaching new and how is it related to commanding unclean spirits? Maybe an answer to these questions will help us to better understand the authority of Jesus' teaching.

Jesus' instruction is not as diverse in Mark as it is in Matthew and Luke. Up to the messianic confession in Mark 8, the author reports little of the actual teaching of Jesus. What he does report, however, falls into two categories. Some teaching is solicited by some or other controversy. Mark 7:1-23 provides a good example. But it is the other type of teaching—that which is not given in response to an accusation or a question—that best indicates the general content of Jesus' message and fits the context of Mark 1:22. In the first half of Mark, the unsolicited teaching of Jesus concerns exclusively the kingdom. Jesus teaches concerning the mystery of the kingdom (Mark 4:13). He announces that the kingdom of God is at hand (Mark 1:15; 4:16, 30); now is the time to repent (Mark 1:15; 2:17; 6:12).

This unity to Jesus' teaching can be seen in the way that the author used "the word" (*ho logos*) as an absolute for Jesus' message (Mark 2:2; 4:33). The author's intention is clear. Mark's Jesus is not a new Moses handing down a book of laws. Rather, he is God's Son who has come announcing the good news of the kingdom.[13]

But in what way is this teaching new? As I have already indicated, it is not really the content of the message which is new. Rather, Jesus' teaching is new in that through it Jesus calls the kingdom into being.

There are two points which I wish to make. The first concerns the connection in Mark between Jesus' teaching and his mighty acts. I have already noted that Jesus' teaching in Mark 1:22-27 is directly connected to his act of exorcizing the unclean spirit. But this actually represents something of a pattern in Mark. For instance, the teaching in Mark 4:2-34 is followed by Jesus' activity of calming the storm (Mark 4:35-41), and the teaching in Mark 11:15-18 is accompanied by Jesus' activity of cleansing the temple.

This pattern of teaching and acting is even more evident when reference is made to "the word" of Jesus. In Mark 2:2 the evangelist joined Jesus' preaching of "the word" to the healing of the paralytic (Mark 2:3-12), and in Mark 4:33-34 "the word" actually provides the transition from the parables (Mark 4:1-32) into the miracle of the calming of the storm (Mark 4:35-41). But there is already a better example of this pattern in the first chapter of Mark where Jesus' mission of preaching in the synagogues is linked to casting out demons.

> And he said to them, "Let us go on to the next towns, that I may preach there also; for that is why I came out." And he went throughout all Galilee preaching in their synagogues and casting out demons (Mark 1:38-39)

After this introduction, Jesus heals a man with leprosy who then in turn goes out himself and begins to preach and spread "the word" (*ho de exelthōn erxato keryssein polla kai diaphēmizein ton logon,* Mark 1:45). The clear sense in Mark is that the miracles give evidence to the inbreaking kingdom. This supports Kee's suggestion that the kingdom can be seen as having drawn near through the exorcisms.[14] The background of the exorcisms is not to be found in the christological question, "Who is Jesus?" but in the eschatological question, "How is God regaining control over an estranged creation?"[15]

But there is something more to the authority of Jesus' teaching—and this is my second point. The kingdom is being created by "the word." It is being called into being by Jesus' teaching—which brings about the new world. It is a well-known aspect of Jewish and early Christian wisdom that "the word" was considered to be a creative force.[16] Actually, one need to go no further than the prologue to the Gospel of John or the creation story in Genesis where God gives order to the world through his word to sense the importance of this concept to Jewish and Christian thought.

The most extensive account of Jesus' teaching in the first half of Mark also calls upon this conceptual heritage—but with special reference to the kingdom of God. In Mark 4 Jesus teaches about the mystery of the kingdom by telling the parable of the sower (Mark 4:3-9). Then, he explains the parable by indicating that the seed which the sower casts out is actually "the word." Although in the popular Christianity of our day, it is common to think of "the word" as the good news of Jesus' life and death, in Jesus' speech, "the word" indicates the good news of the kingdom which is arriving (see Mark 4:30-33). But for our purposes, what is significant here is that it is "the word" itself that when sown on good soil brings forth fruit (Mark 4:20). The news of the kingdom mysteriously brings forth the kingdom.

Jesus' mighty acts in Mark—the miracles and exorcisms—are manifestations of Jesus' teaching. What is new about Jesus' teaching is that the teaching itself, "the word," brings about the full harvest. In turn, the answer to Jesus' authority in Mark is also to be found in his miracles—but not in that they point to Jesus' person. The miracles signify his teaching. Authority (*exousia*) in Mark 1:22 is perhaps better translated by "power." Jesus' teaching has power because it brings about the new age. Whereas the scribes hoped for the kingdom and spoke about it, Jesus' teaching brought it into being.

III. The Authority of Jesus' Teaching for Our Day

The authority of Jesus' teaching is often made to refer to the poles law and liberty. Thus, it is common to ask about the basis, the character, and the permanence of Jesus' teaching. Does the teaching indicate a means of winning God's favor or a response of gratitude? Does the teaching embody timeless norms or does it consist of historically and socially conditioned directions for living? Does the teaching represent an eternal order that will continue into the Age to Come, or does it possess only provisional and this-worldly significance?[17]

But these questions are completely misleading when applied to Jesus' teaching at the beginning of Mark. There, Jesus does not give us a body of material that can be appropriated as a guide to proper conduct. The teaching is neither a means of winning God's favor nor a response to God's grace; it does not embody norms, either timeless or timely; and it does not represent an eternal or a temporal order. Jesus' teaching is the power of God that is giving birth to the new creation.

And perhaps it is here that Mark speaks with special significance for our day. It seems to me that both the conservative and liberal traditions in American Christianity have coalesced in their view of Jesus' teaching. They have joined in holding too closely to the paradigm of the textbook, that is, in thinking of Jesus' teaching almost exclusively as a body of knowledge to be passed from one generation to the next, to be appropriated and put to use.

Of course the method of taking hold of the teaching has been debated, with liberals favoring critical tools to uncover the message of Jesus, while conservatives hold to an entrenched position of biblical inerrancy or church tradition. Also, the content of the teaching has been evaluated differently, for instance with liberals perhaps more emphatic in their pro-life stand against capital punishment and conservatives more emphatic in their pro-life stand against abortion. But, on the whole liberals and conservatives have agreed that Jesus' teaching is a type of guideline for daily living.

They have also found some common ground in the belief that Jesus' teaching presents an agenda for tomorrow's kingdom. Again, the blueprint for the future in the liberal community sharply contrasts with the blueprint in the conservative community. Whereas liberals seem to emphasize that people were made in the image of God and draw attention to the brotherhood and reasonableness of people everywhere, conservatives seem to emphasize the alienation of this world from God. The blueprint in the conservative tradition is more likely to take the form of apocalyptic or separation from the secular world, and in the liberal tradition, social gospel or the transformation of the world.

But in regard to the authority of Jesus' teaching, it is the similarity between conservative and liberal which is so significant and disturbing. Both hold to a static view of revelation which locks Jesus and his teaching tightly into the past. To the liberal community, Jesus is the great teacher who always practiced what he taught. He is the supreme example for men and women to follow. To the conservative community, Jesus is the king or the great lawgiver, who with divine insight gave future generations a set of rules by which to live. In either case God is removed from history—or better, he is no longer allowed to act in a new way in our world. At best, he is allowed to act in an indirect way, influencing humanity by what he did in the past.

Can God in fact speak a new word for our age? Is he concerned with our problems of space exploration, nuclear proliferation, and in-vitro fertilization? One of the purposes of theology is to make clear the embarrassment of people when confronted with the living God. Perhaps, Mark 1:22 can help our generation remember that Jesus' teaching had authority exactly because it represented God's activity in Capernaum's present. While the scribes located God in the past, Jesus' teaching signified the presence of God in the modern world.

Notes

1. J. Hargreaves, A Guide to St. Mark's Gospel (London: SPCK, 1965), 24; W. Harrington, Mark (Wilmington: Michael Glazier, 1979), 15-17; C. Leslie-Mitton, The Gospel According to Mark (London: Epworth, 1957), 10-11; A. Loisy, L'Évangile selon Marc (Paris: Émile Nourry, 1912), 70-1; V. K. Robbins, Jesus the Teacher (Philadelphia: Fortress, 1984), 118; E. Schweizer, The Good News According to Mark (Richmond: John Knox, 1970), 51; A.

Sledd, *Saint Mark's Life of Jesus* (Nashville: Cokesbury, 1927), 35-36; E. T. Thompson, *The Gospel According to Mark and its Meaning for Today* (Richmond: John Knox, 1954), 46; and A. N. Wilder, *Eschatology and Ethics in the Teaching of Jesus* (Westport: Greenwood, 1950), 163-75.

2. D. Daube, "*Exousia* in Mark I:22 and 27." *JTS* 39 (1938): 45-59.

3. A. W. Argyle, "The Meaning of *exousia* in Mark i.22, 27." *ExpT* 80 (1968-69): 343.

4. E. Schweizer, "Mark's Contribution to the Quest of the Historical Jesus," *NTS* 10 (1963-64): 422-23.

5. P. S. Minear, *Matthew: The Teacher's Gospel* (New York: Pilgrim), 45-60.

6. P. Guillemette, "Un Enseignement Nouveau, Plein D'Autorité," *NovT* 12 (1980): 239.

7. D. Abernathy, *Understanding the Teaching of Jesus* (New York: Seabury, 1983), 46.

8. Guillemette, 240.

9. A. T. Hanson, *The Living Utterances of God* (London: Darton, Longman, and Todd, 1983), 20-36.

10. D. E. Trueblood, *The Humor of Christ* (New York: Harper & Row, 1975), 90-92.

11. H. C. Kee, "The Terminology of Mark's Exorcism Stories," *NTS* 14 (1967-68): 242: and D. Dideberg and P. M. Beernaert, "Jesus vint en Galilée," *Nouvelle Revue Théologique* 98 (1976): 313.

12. Kee, 242.

13. E. Käsemann, *New Testament Questions of Today* (Philadelphia: Fortress, 1969), 80-81.

14. Kee, 242.

15. Ibid., 246.

16. A. N. Wilder, *Early Christian Rhetoric* (Cambridge: Harvard, 1976), 7.

17. R. Banks, *Jesus and the Law in the Synoptic Tradition* (London: Cambridge, 1975), 13.

Authority According to St. Francis: Power or Powerlessness?

3

Wayne Hellmann

Department of Theological Studies
St. Louis University

FOR ALL PRACTICAL PURPOSES the notion of authority does not enter into the thought or vocabulary of St. Francis of Assisi. An examination of his writings reveals that he uses the word "authority" only once, in speaking of the wives of those whose husbands wish to join the fraternity. St. Francis says that wives may give their husbands' permission to join the fraternity by the authority of the bishop of the diocese.[1] In speaking of authority, then, there is nothing about it which pertains to the professed life and obedience of the brothers.

St. Francis does employ the word "obedience." It appears forty-eight times in his writings. Throughout the collection of admonitions, letters, and rules which make up the writings of St. Francis, the relationship of the brothers to one another "in obedience" is deemed a prized gospel value. According to St. Francis, the brothers are to obey each other, their ministers, "the Lord Pope Honorius and his canonically elected successors and the Roman Church."[2]

This essay commences by examining the structure of the brotherhood established by St. Francis, beginning with the office of the minister. Ministers are not to lord it over the other brothers but are at the service of all the friars. Those in charge of the fraternity are not to be power-hungry but are there to serve the others.

Although St. Francis hardly mentions the word "authority," he does have a lot to say about "obedience." This term describes well the rule and life of the friars. Obedience does not exist by itself, but ought to be considered in connection with love. Love is the true basis of both obedience and authority as we shall see in the final section of our essay.

I. Office of the Minister

A clear structure exists within the brotherhood founded by St. Francis. There are the ministers who alone may receive new brothers into the fraternity, and all the brothers who are bound to "diligently obey them."[3] The ministers assign the brothers to the various places and approve them for various offices. "And none of the brothers shall dare to preach to the people unless he has been examined and approved by the minister general of this fraternity and has received from him the office of preaching."[4] The ministers function on different levels. There is the general minister for the whole fraternity and the provincial minister for the provinces. Toward the end of his life, with the development of the new religious order, there evolved the guardians or local ministers who served in the various places the brothers dwell.

The new fraternity has a structure which is shared by other orders, but in the formation of this structure Francis introduces new language and gives new meaning to its purpose. He avoids the monastic use of the term "abbot"; and he makes it clear that "no one should be called Prior, but all generally should be called Friars Minor. And the one should wash the feet of the others."[5] All the brothers are to serve each other. What all the brothers are and what all the brothers do is precisely what the ministers are to be and to do. The ministers are first and foremost brothers. "All the brothers who have been established as ministers and servants of the other brothers . . . should visit them frequently and spiritually admonish and encourage them."[6] Among the brothers, some are called to visit and encourage the others. The relationship of those who are the ministers to the other brothers is primarily fraternal. The need for service to the brothers is the reason for the office of minister. In fact, in chapter 10 of the *Later Rule,* Francis explicitly writes that the brothers should be able to "speak and deal with the ministers as masters with their servants; for this is the way it should be: The ministers shall be the servants of all the brothers."[7]

Service is primary. *The Fourth Admonition* is directed entirely to those who serve as ministers. The focus is on the text of Matthew's Gospel which speaks of service (Matt 10:28). If, indeed, service characterizes a minister, then ministers can glory in their office only insofar as they can glory in washing the feet of others. Otherwise, their service is not a ministry of the gospel. Ministry is the office of washing feet. If such is not their attitude, their office is not salvific for them and they can lose their souls. In his perceptive insight into human nature, Francis sees that real attitudes are revealed when one is asked to give up an office. It is sufficient to quote the *Fourth Admonition* in full:

> I did not come to be served but to serve (cf. Matt 10:28), says the Lord. Those who are placed over others should glory in such an office only as much as they would were they assigned the task of washing the feet of the brothers. And the more they are upset about their office being taken from them than they would be over the loss of the office of washing feet, so much the more do they store up treasures to the peril of their souls (cf. John 12:6).[8]

Service as the office of the minister cannot be rooted in one's own will. The test of this is the constant readiness to lay down the office. Once it becomes a possession it is spiritually dangerous. The key to St. Francis's whole spirituality is this: that the brothers may refer nothing to themselves. Anything which can provide power or status must be referred to God. This is true for the office of preaching, the office of minister, and even for those who have knowledge of the Sacred Scripture: "And those are given life by the spirit of Sacred Scripture who do not refer to themselves any text which they know or seek to know, but, by word and example, return everything to the most high Lord God to Whom every good belongs."[9]

Furthermore, "we must never desire to be over others; rather we must be servants and subject to every human creature for God's sake."[10] This applies to the ministers as well. Although the other brothers are subject to the ministers, the ministers are not above them. The ministers are likewise subject to the other brothers, who in turn are subject to them. Just as the ministers must admonish and correct the brothers, so are they to be admonished and corrected. The brothers are to keep careful watch over the ministers:

> Nonetheless, all the brothers, who are subject to the ministers and servants, should reasonably and diligently consider the actions of the ministers and servants. And if they should see that any of them is living according to the flesh and not according to the Spirit—as demanded for the integrity of our life—if he does not amend his way, after a third admonition they should inform the minister and servant of the whole fraternity at the Chapter of Pentecost without any interference or opposition.[11]

Much of what Francis writes concerning the duties of the minister as servant is precisely what he sees as fundamental to the fraternal relationships of all the brothers. The brothers are to obey the ministers, but all the brothers are "to serve and obey one another."[12] The minister "should use and show mercy to each of his brothers as he would wish

them to do to him were he in a similar position."[13] Concerning a sick
or needy brother, Francis also writes that all the brothers are "to serve
him as they would wish to be served themselves."[14] The model which
emerges for the minister develops simply from what all the brothers are
to do. One could say the minister is a brother *par excellence.* He is
indeed a brother called to serve, not by his own will and not as a
prerogative that belongs to him. Rather, he who accepts this office is
to do so with responsibility because "if anyone of them should be lost
because of their fault and bad example, these ministers and servants
will have to render an account before the Lord Jesus Christ on the day
of judgment."[15]

For Francis, there can be no greater fault in a minister than clinging
to power. Repeatedly he admonishes: "And let the ministers and servants remember what the Lord says: I have not come to be served but
to serve."[16] Power is contrary to the service of others. It is rather service
to self. It is forbidden for all the brothers to hold power of dominion;
and this of course includes the ministers. Perhaps this is why Francis
avoids the use of the word "authority" when speaking of the office of
the minister. In his age, as well as in our own, authority is associated
with power, and this is forbidden them because it is contrary to the
Gospel words of our Lord:

> Similarly, all the brothers in this regard should not hold power or dominion,
> least of all among themselves. For, as the Lord says in the Gospel: The rulers
> of the peoples have power over them (Matt 20:25); it shall not be like this
> among the brothers (cf. Matt 20:26a). And whoever among them wishes to
> become greater should be their minister (cf. Matt 20:26b) and servant. And
> whoever is the greater among them should become like the lesser (cf. Luke
> 22:26).[17]

II. Relationship of Obedience

"When the year of probation is ended let them be received into obedience."[18] This is how acceptance into the brotherhood is described.
Authority may not be mentioned in Francis's writings when he speaks
of the ministers, but obedience is a fundamental description of the rule
and life of the Friars Minor. Obedience is not, therefore, a simple
response to authority. It is rather the way the brothers "return everything
to the most high Lord God to whom every good belongs."[19]

Francis's vision of obedience is primarily that of a proper relationship
to the Lord. The basic sin of Adam was one of disobedience, and a

life of obedience is that which undoes Adam's sin in us and destroys
its power:

> He was able to eat of every tree of paradise since he did not sin as long as
> he did not go against obedience. For the person eats of the tree of the
> knowledge of good who appropriates to himself his own will and thus exalts
> himself over the good things which the Lord says and does in him; and thus,
> through the suggestion of the devil and the transgression of the command,
> what he eats becomes for him the fruit of the knowledge of evil. Therefore
> it is necessary that he bear the punishment.[20]

Obedience is disappropriation of one's own will to the extent that
clinging to one's will is the self-appropriation of God's power and
goodness. Obedience renounces power because it recognizes that power
belongs to God alone. Francis warns those brothers (who have been
received into obedience in order to undo the power of sin), to beware
lest they "return to the vomit of their own will."[21] For Francis, obedience
is not a response to authority. Rather, it is a way of salvation and
liberation which enables the brother to refer all good to the Lord.
Obedience claims nothing. Obedience is rather a recognition of "the
most high Lord God to whom every good belongs."[22]

The brothers' relationship to God, however, is lived out concretely
and incarnationally in their relationship to each other. There cannot
be the appropriation of one's own will in a mutual relationship. There
is no other way they can be lesser brothers unless they obey one another.
"And blessed is that servant who does not place himself in a high
position of his own will and always desires to be under the feet of
others."[23] The focus in this is "our Lord Jesus Christ who gave His life
that He might not lose the obedience of the most holy Father."[24]

The obedience of our Lord Jesus Christ is total self-surrender. He
teaches the way of obedience as he undoes the sin of Adam in us. The
brothers are to do the same as our Lord, and they are to do this in
their mutual relationships and in their relationship to their ministers.
The *Third Admonition* uses the exceptional word, "prelate," instead of
minister, and indicates, thereby, the influence of some help in the
writing of this admonition, but the core of the message is definitely
Francis:

> But if the prelate should command something contrary to his conscience,
> although the subject does not obey him, still he should not abandon him.
> And if in consequence he suffers persecution from others, let him love them
> even more for the love of God. For whoever chooses to endure persecution
> rather than be separated from his brothers truly remains in perfect obedience
> for he lays down his life (John 15:13) for his brothers.[25]

Self-surrender characterizes the relationship of the friar to God as well as his relationship to his minister. Self-surrender (which involves giving up all that one possesses, including one's freedom) is simply another term for obedience. However, this obedience is not blind or without conditions. Obedience must be salvific and the undoing of sin. The brother always obeys his minister "provided that what he does is good" and that it is "not contrary to his conscience." Obedience has a positive content for Francis. It means doing good and it is conscience which reveals the good. However, even in the case in which the brother cannot obey his minister "still he should not abandon him." That would not be good. Such a situation can call for suffering and can even be the occasion for a greater and more profound obedience. Even when the brother cannot obey, he cannot sever the mutual relationship of the brotherhood, for without the brotherhood there can be no obedience. In this case, a severance would be self-appropriation which is the primary sin, disobedience. Rather, the suffering involved in maintaining the relationship when one cannot obey is a greater obedience.

Francis sees obedience as fundamental and basic to his fraternity. He speaks of it on the level of salvation because obedience undoes sin. He understands the general relationship of the brothers as one of obedience because this allows them to be "lesser" to each other. In the fraternal relationship, the ministers serve the brothers in many ways, but they serve them clearly in their life of obedience to each other and to the Lord. Francis's *Letter to Brother Leo* is the *Magna Carta* of Franciscan obedience. Francis encourages Leo, "In whatever way it seems best to you to please the Lord God and follow His footprints and His poverty, do this with the blessing of God and my obedience."[26]

This is precisely, however, where obedience is conditioned and limited. When he writes that the brothers are to obey the ministers, they should obey only "in those matters which concern the well-being of their soul and which are not contrary to our life."[27] He explicitly states that "should any of the ministers command any of the brothers to do something contrary to our life or against his conscience, he is not bound to obey him, since that is not obedience in which a fault is committed.[28] The minister is to facilitate the doing of good among the brothers which will "please the Lord God."[29] This good can only be in the total context of the gospel life the brothers have promised to observe. Any obedience outside the way of the gospel life and contrary to the dictates of one's conscience does not really qualify as obedience.

The minister has no power. He can only minister and facilitate gospel obedience, an obedience which is fundamentally fraternal. The minister can call the brothers forth to obey "in all those things which they have promised the Lord."[30] Indeed, the ministers should "charitably correct them, not commanding them anything which might be against their conscience and our Rule. On the other hand, the brothers who are subject to them should remember that they have given up their own wills for God."[31]

There is a beautiful balance in Francis's vision. Gospel obedience limits the ministers by the consciences of the brothers and by the Rule. The freedom of the brothers is protected that they might live the Rule they have promised and that they might live the inner light of their consciences. Yet, the brothers are called to be faithful to the fact that they have given up their own wills for God. This ensures that they will not exalt self "over the good things which the Lord says and does" in them.[32] The brothers' obedience to one another and to the ministers in particular is the acceptance of a ministry which is the salvific undoing of the power of sin in both the minister and the brother. This kind of obedience frees one from self and opens the door to new relationships which do not need status, position, or power. Obedience on the part of all the brothers allows them all, ministers and the other brothers, to be indeed "lesser" brothers.

III. Conclusion

Precisely in an age of canonical developments in law and clerical structures of authority in the church, Francis offers an alternative vision that goes much deeper. It is astounding that he can write so profusely of obedience without the need to mention authority. Even in his "obedience and reverence to the Lord Pope Honorius"[33] he mentions nothing about papal authority. Rather his concern is that in mutual gospel obedience there is the undoing of the basic sin of lust for power. A brotherhood emerges in which no one has power or dominion over the other. Gospel authority is powerlessness, and this is where there is true fraternal obedience, one where the friars offer their own wills to God.

The power experienced in obedience cannot be the power of one will over another, but it is rather the power of love. Love is the only genuine authority because as Francis writes in chapter 5 of his *Earlier Rule*, it is "through the charity of the Spirit, they should voluntarily serve and obey one another. And this is the true and holy obedience of our Lord Jesus Christ."[34]

Notes

1. *Later Rule*, ch. 2 in: *The Writings of Francis and Clare*, transl. by R. Armstrong and I. Brady (Ramsey, N.J.: Paulist, 1982), 138. All references to the writings of St. Francis are taken from this translation of the critical texts. *Opuscula Sancti Patris Francisci Assiensis*, ed. K. Esser, O.F.M. (Grottaferrata: Grottaferrata Publishers, 1978).

2. *Later Rule*, 138.
3. *Earlier Rule*, ch. 4, 112.
4. *Later Rule*, ch. 9, 143.
5. *Earlier Rule*, ch. 6, 114.
6. Ibid., ch. 4, 112.
7. *Later Rule*, ch. 10, 143.
8. *Fourth Admonition*, 28.
9. *Seventh Admonition*, 30.
10. *The Second Version of the Letter to the Faithful*, 70.
11. *Earlier Rule*, ch. 5, 113.
12. Ibid., ch. 5, 114.
13. *The Second Version of the Letter to the Faithful*, 70.
14. *Earlier Rule*, ch. 10, 118.
15. Ibid., ch. 4, 113.
16. Ibid., ch. 4, 112-13.
17. Ibid., ch. 5, 113-14.
18. *Later Rule*, ch. 2, 138.
19. *Seventh Admonition*, 30.
20. *Second Admonition*, 27.
21. *Third Admonition*, 28.
22. *Seventh Admonition*, 30.
23. *Nineteenth Admonition*, 33.
24. *A Letter to the Entire Order*, 60.
25. *Third Admonition*, 28.
26. *A Letter to Brother Leo*, 48.
27. *Earlier Rule*, ch. 4, 112.
28. Ibid., ch. 5, 113.
29. *A Letter to Leo*, 48.
30. *Later Rule*, ch. 10, 143.
31. Ibid.
32. *Second Admonition*, 27.
33. *Later Rule*, ch. 1, 137.
34. *Earlier Rule*, ch. 5, 114.

Re-Thinking Authority: Imaginative Options and the Modernist Controversy

4

Jo Ann Eigelsbach

Columbia, Maryland

ANY ATTEMPT TO CRITICIZE or to reform without sufficient depth of understanding is an exercise in futility. The current crisis in authority in the Roman Catholic Church did not arise in a vacuum, but is the product of a complex history of ideas and events.

In the present situation, many recognize the necessity of reestablishing the place of authority in community and consensus, and some authors use as their frame of reference a vision of the New Testament or of the early church as a "golden age." The insight dissolves into romantic nostalgia if left at that. The present situation has a history that cannot be ignored by anyone serious about reform, and its complexity calls for analytical tools that can address its sociological, political, economic, cultural, and philosophical dimensions.

A critical period in the history of the issue of authority was the nineteenth century, a time when the papacy struggled for power and identity amid the social upheavals and political realignment of Europe, and when new currents of thought challenged the assumptions and conclusions of an ahistorical scholastic philosophy.

Behind every choice, every movement for change or reform, lies a spectrum of imaginative options. What is chosen and acted upon must first be conceived as possible; what is not envisioned as within the range of possibility cannot be chosen. In hopes of a deeper understanding, the historian can bring to light the assumptions that lay behind concrete historical options and the imaginative frameworks out of which they emerged. This is the world, or the horizon of the past, and it does not stand in isolation, but in an ongoing history of contexts that shape the assumptions and imaginative framework in which the historical options of our own time may be understood.

In view of the larger project of historical understanding and critical analysis, this essay examines the late-nineteenth century perspective of author and Newmanite Wilfrid Philip Ward. Bernard Lonergan's description of the dialectic of authority from community to institutional complexity and Matthew Lamb's discussion of pluralist political dialectics will assist this endeavor in analyzing the issue of authority in Ward's time and in our own.

I. The Intelligibility of Authority

Authority is legitimate power.[1] The ultimate source of power is cooperation and consensus in communities in the present and in history. Authority resides in communities, i.e., groups united by common experience, understanding, judgments, and goals. As social organization becomes more complex, authority brings the achievements of the past into the present, organizes and directs the hierarchy of cooperating groups, distributes the fruits of cooperation, and excludes disruptive elements. Commonly understood and accepted patterns of cooperation evolve, comprising institutions within which individuals are designated as authorities: leaders in times of stress; judges in disputes; and other functionaries.

The Dialectic of Authority

The legitimacy of authority depends on the authenticity of the common meanings and values of the tradition and of persons and communities at each level and stage in the process. Authenticity is never a secure once-for-all achievement. The way authority is exercised in a community can promote or restrict responsible human freedom and its self-corrective process.

At any level and stage in the development of the tradition the option of inauthenticity is possible and the inauthentic response can become part of the common heritage of knowledge and policies. The structures of authority established in the community promote the self-corrective process of responsible human freedom when they allow the questions to be raised that would allow the fruits of inattentiveness, misunderstanding, irrationality, and irresponsibility to be revealed and corrected.

When the established authority structures within the community impose and reinforce systems of thought and action so that the natural self-corrective process of human intelligence is impeded, authority promotes inauthenticity in the tradition and at the same time calls its own legitimacy into question. When this situation becomes extreme, revolutionary change that would dismantle and reorganize the structures of the community may be the recourse of those who seek to recover the authenticity of the tradition, and their response, in turn, would have its own possibilities of authenticity or inauthenticity.

The dialectic of authority is the complex and concrete interaction of authenticity and inauthenticity in the community as a whole, in its designated authorities, and in the individuals subject to those authorities. In a global view, it appears in the conflict between an institutional ideal and its imperfect realizations. The exercise of authority in a particular historical situation includes a complex and dynamic combination of authenticity and inauthenticity.

Lonergan's framework outlines the development of the function of authority from simple to complex, from community to institution. This provides a tool for analyzing the dialectic of authority in particular situations, and it establishes a starting point for discussion. It also provides a frame of reference for the historian's understanding of authority, which, although bracketed in the attempt to reveal Ward's particular horizon as expressed in his own terms, nevertheless operates as background to the telling of the story that cannot be ignored. The frame of reference once again becomes explicit when the historian wants to move out of the story to reflect, analyze, make comparisons, draw conclusions, and to invite dialogue and criticism.

II. Wilfrid Ward

Wilfrid Philip Ward, a key figure in English Roman Catholicism from 1882 to 1916, was the son of the famous Ultramontane W. G. Ward. He dissociated himself from his father's views and became the disciple of Newman, interpreting Newman's vision of the church for a troubled time. On the one hand, he saw the necessity of authority and viewed the principle of authority in the church as the bulwark of social order. He also realized the critical importance of grounding the principle of religious authority in terms intelligible to modern science and philosophy. On the other hand, he recognized the need for reform. From Newman he derived a model that would allow for gradual reform without endangering the necessary principle of authority.

The heart of Ward's life and work was his preoccupation with a twofold challenge to Catholic faith: from without, the spread of agnosticism and skepticism; and, from within, the necessity of reform. At a time when Catholic writers usually appealed to a small, intellectually isolated audience, Ward's essays presented the case for the intellectual credibility of theism and of Roman Catholicism in the public forum of the most prestigious periodicals of his time. His biographies of W. G. Ward, Cardinal Wiseman, and Cardinal Newman are noted for their excellence. As editor of *The Dublin Review*, the leading Catholic period-ical in England, he broadened its scope and readership.

Ward believed that inevitable and necessary reform was best intro-duced in the context of an historical understanding of the fundamental principles of Christianity, which included adaptation to changing philosophical and cultural contexts. In this way, revolutionary changes could be accomplished with a minimum of disruption to people's spiritual lives. His popular essays and reviews offered a view of Christianity in an historical, evolutionary framework that was designed to establish a context for understanding the changes necessary in the contemporary situation.

III. Authority: Ward's Spectrum of Options

Protestant Liberalism

Ward had an ongoing quarrel with the Protestant liberal position represented by Matthew Arnold and Arnold's niece, novelist Mrs. Humphrey Ward. To Ward, they represented a second and third gen-eration of the attitude of the Oxford Noetics, who accepted no authority and subjected all premises to the questioning of individual reason.[2] The loss of the guiding principle of authority which counterbalanced the skeptical tendencies of individual reason had ultimately led to agnosti-cism or an unacceptable "Reduced Christianity."[3]

Ahistorical Scholasticism

The scholastic theology of Wilfrid Ward's seminary days offered little that would achieve credibility with the broader intellectual public that Ward addressed. It defensively over-emphasized the role of authority and presented it almost as an end in itself, detached from the workings of other elements in the church. Authority was legitimated by an argument that Jesus, by miracles and the resurrection, proved his claim to divine authority, which he delegated to the church, handing over supernatural truths and promising the guidance of the Holy Spirit. Such supernatural legitimations, and their direct connection to the status quo, became problematic in the light of biblical and historical criticism.[4]

Ultramontanism

Wilfrid Ward's father, W. G. Ward, became famous for the jest that he would like to see a Papal Bull each day at breakfast with the *Times*.[5] In the course of his intellectual journey from the liberalism of Thomas and Matthew Arnold to the Oxford Movement and eventually to Roman Catholicism, he became convinced that the independent intellect needed restraint and guidance, and that without them, pessimism and skepticism were inevitable. For him, the authority of Rome was indispensable. A large number of infallible utterances was desirable, constituting firm ground in the midst of skepticism and agnosticism. He championed the Ultramontane cause in the debates of the 1860s and 1870s.

However, while recognizing the *principle* of authority revered by the Ultramontanes as the stopgap against intellectual and social chaos, his son, Wilfrid Ward, objected to the canonization of its particular historical forms and the exaltation of papal authority detached from its roots in the dynamics of the tradition. For Wilfrid Ward, the options of Ultramontanism, scholasticism, and Protestant liberalism were unacceptable. He found in Newman the key to an adequate understanding of the proper relationship between authority and individual reason.

Newman

Ward's analysis of the church, inspired by Newman, grounded the principle of a central authority in the common experience of the need to preserve group identity and continuity. He saw the need for the power of definitive judgment of conflicting interpretations of tradition — in Ward's view, an important advantage of the Roman Church over the Anglican, where no one party could claim to speak for the church. He located the function of authority in the process of historical development, understood as a dynamic of resistance and assimilation. And he ultimately located the intelligibility of authority and of infallibility in the context of spirituality.[6]

IV. The Necessity and Character of Authority

According to Ward, the *Catholic* principle of central authority contrasted with the *Protestant* principle of private judgment. It represented the time-honored wisdom of tradition in contrast to the assertions of individual reason. The excesses of individual reason set loose by the Enlightenment had become a disintegrating force in society, and the

corrective of authority was needed. The wisdom of the Christian tradition safeguarded in the Roman Catholic Church by the principle of
authority, was, for Newman and for Ward, the only viable alternative
to the forces of atheism and secularism.[7] Ward offered his interpretation
of a commonplace theory of sets of mutually conditioning orders,
namely, those of church and society. The order of society depended
on morality, and morality ultimately depended on religious conviction,
engendered and supported by the structures of the institutional church.
The integrity of the Christian tradition could only be maintained by
the authority and discipline that the Roman Catholic Church alone
had preserved.

Authority and Reason

Authority was the necessary and natural counterweight to individual
reason. Ward, following Newman, understood reason as a secondary
operation working from the basis of first principles but not establishing
them. When individual reason tried to prove or establish first principles,
skepticism was the inevitable result. He pointed out that "free" reason
usually uncritically operated out of the reigning secularist and naturalist
assumptions of the culture.[8] Authority, as the articulation of the wisdom
of tradition, provided first principles and set the terms within which
reason could successfully operate.[9]

Ward intended to move beyond positions that placed authority and
reason in opposition, exalting one to the deprecation of the other.[10]
Authority was the embodiment of "the reason of the race," and there
was a mutually corrective relation between the individual reason and
authority.

> . . .the reasoning of one generation naturally issues in conclusions which
> form the "groundwork" of social life for the individuals in the next. And in
> this way a very few achievements of the individual Reason come to affect
> the whole race; and the successful struggle of Reason against Authority in
> one generation may issue in a change in the "groundwork" which is due to
> Reason, although it does not necessarily affect all individuals through the
> medium of their own reasoning faculties.[11]

The role of the individual reason was to test in a limited way, to use,
and to correct the larger fund of knowledge. The test of authority was
a practical one, and practical certainty and trust in authority came
from the gain in fruitfulness and coherence that the knowledge in
question gave to individual experience.

Authority in the Context of Ward's Apologetics

Ward developed arguments that represented a new approach to

apologetics, grounding belief in concrete experience rather than in abstract logic. He shifted the terms of the discussion from proof to practical certainty, and regarded the act of belief as an integrated process of action and reflection rather than the function of a detached reason.

Ward's apologetics for authority had a commonsense, practical basis. His concept of authority always had experiential and historical connotations and never meant the absolute reign of "officialism."[12] Recognition of the existence of and need for authority could be gained from the observation of the interaction of communities and individuals in everyday life.[13] Authority represented the cumulative and enduring wisdom that outweighed the narrow range of knowledge available to personal experience. It made sense for the individual to make use of such a resource, and so the acceptance of authority could be a rational choice.

Ward distinguished blind trust from the intelligent use of authority, which he called "rational trust," and noted that such trust is a normal occurrence in everyday social life. Rational trust was based on the idea that individuals could appreciate a discovery or an expertise and see that it "worked" in practice sufficiently to place trust in the discoverer or expert, without having to repeat the discovery or having the expertise on their own.[14] If individuals found the authority trustworthy on points within the range of their experience, they could reasonably choose to extend that trust to areas beyond.

The individual depended on the expertise of others; in religion this expertise was embodied in the tradition, and authority functioned as the guardian of the tradition. Saints and mystics were the pioneers in religion; their perceptions were fully developed, whereas those of others were primitive. It was possible to place a rational trust in their vision and counsel as embodied in religious traditions.

For Ward, church authority was a specific instance of a general function necessary for the identity and continuity of any organization.

> All civilized communities draw up, as they grow, with increasing precision, the rules which experience shows to be necessary for their preservation. . . . The difficulties in allowing such claims . . . are difficulties not against modern Rome only, but against the action of the Christian Church from the first, in preserving unity of polity and doctrine by the exclusion of heresy.[15]

History demonstrated that the necessity of authority was simply a practical one. In contrast to the ahistorical emphasis on authority in the theology he studied as a seminarian, Ward viewed the function of authority within the evolutionary dynamics of tradition. It did not function alone or arbitrarily, but as one element in relation to others in a larger process.

Authority in an Evolutionary Context

The value of church authority was derived from its function in the process of the development of the tradition. Ward's view of the progress of the church involved an interaction of thinkers, saints, and rulers, representing the interests of truth, devotion, and stable rule. Each of these groups in its own way represented the corporate authority of the church.[16] Rulers guarded the tradition established by the saints, and thinkers advanced the wisdom of the church by their creative intellect. Ward envisioned a balance of the mystical, intellectual, and governing functions comprising what he termed "the constitution of the Church."[17] Ward described the dynamic of the church's development as one of *resistance and assimilation*. Resistance was the function of authority, and assimilation was the task of individuals, who carefully tested new theories. Ward's concern was for peaceful transitions in the process of development; both conservation and experimentation were necessary. Before the Modernist episode, he thought that if the preservation of the unity of faith must take precedence over intellectual advances in certain conflict situations, the assimilative principle would guarantee the eventual restoration of equilibrium. Later, he qualified the latitude he allowed for restraint.

The Uses and Abuses of Authority

In view of the balance of functions, Ward argued for both intellectual freedom and restraint, insisting that the power of restraint must be exercised with prudent judgment and that the role of church authority in intellectual matters necessitated consulting theological experts. In Ward's view, abuses of authority were ultimately self-destructive.

> To reject what is not mere brilliant speculation but is the practically unanimous verdict of the scholars, is unnecessary persecution; it may chasten a few, but many will rebel and feel that they have right on their side. The point comes at which submission of the human intellect amounts to a denial to it even of such powers as make a *rationabile obsequium* to the Church herself possible or reliable. Thus authority in forcing its prerogative may undermine the whole of its own basis.[18]

Ward also made it clear that he saw room for the functional adaptation of authority to differing circumstances, but allowed no compromise on the *principle* of authority. At the time of the discussion in the 1890s of Anglican-Roman Catholic Reunion he wrote:

> There may have to be great changes within the church before the separated bodies can again recognize her. But if no other principle, except that which she has retained, can ultimately withstand the inroads of religious negation, may we not hope that forces on all sides will eventually tend towards the desired reunion? The central Authority, as a fact, and not a mere name, is an essential part of the Church thus conceived. But its practical claims and action may vary in the future as they have in the past.[19]

While Ward's theology of the church allowed authority a latitude with which Protestants and more democratically minded Catholics would be uncomfortable, he also brought the rationale for church authority down to earth. The grounding of authority as practical necessity, and its interpretation as a function in dynamic relation to other functions, left its concrete form and exercise open in principle to adaptation and change.

V. Ward's Practical Strategies

Ward's essays were usually occasioned by specific events or contemporary articles or books. During the 1890s ecumenical issues were of central interest, such as the discussion of Anglican Orders and of the attendance of Catholics in the national universities. Ward found himself in an awkward position as both reformer of, and apologist for, Roman Catholicism. To argue for the reasonableness of Rome became difficult after the turn of the century, when the actions of Rome became increasingly defensive. The Joint Pastoral of 1900 and the Encyclical *Pascendi* in 1907 put Ward's views to the test in practical strategies.

The Joint Pastoral of 1900

In 1899, criticism of the actions of the hierarchy in the *Times* by distinguished Catholic scientist St. George Jackson Mivart provoked a controversy that led to his excommunication.[20] Sympathies for Mivart occasioned more outspoken criticisms in the press. Alarmed by this display, Ward hoped a cycle of rebellion and repression could be avoided, and warned "wise liberals" not to provoke authority.[21]

It seemed the cycle was to continue when, on 31 December 1900, the English bishops published a joint pastoral letter that outlined a view of the church divided into two groups, the *ecclesia docens*, the teachers, which included the pope and the bishops, and the *ecclesia discens*, the taught, which included everyone else. Such action disparaged religious thinkers who would presume to instruct the hierarchy.

By 1901 Ward was advising reformers on strategies for a time of repression.[22] The pastoral insisted on the teaching of Vatican I on authority, but omitted the limitations that the Council had introduced. Such an unqualified assertion of the role of authority and the passivity of the laity left no room for Ward's vision of the church or for the work that he espoused.

Ward regarded the pastoral as based on a false analysis of the actual process observable in church history. His response to the pastoral was to avoid direct confrontation, yet go to the root of the problem by offering a more accurate analysis of the process and by interpreting the pastoral in the context of other church documents that would moderate its authoritarian claims.

Having attempted to neutralize the content of the pastoral by outlining its proper context and function, Ward introduced the distinction between the roles of pastors and theologians in a commentary on church history.

> Looking back now at the great *Doctores Ecclesiae*, with the halo round their brows, we may forget to separate their position from that of the pontiffs and bishops who in the long run have sanctioned the results of their labors. But in their own lifetime they did their work not, for the most part, in virtue of any position as members of the *Ecclesia docens*, but prompted by their loyalty, devotion, and genius, and sometimes in spite of opposition on the part of unworthier holders of official status. . . . A great pastor is therefore, not a great Doctor Ecclesiae. . . .It is the select few . . . [theologians who] have been the very life of the Christian Church on the intellectual side, not the crowd of forgotten bishops, many of them excellent rulers, some of them good theologians, but many more of them men of action rather than of thought.[23]

In another article, "Liberalism as a Temper of Mind," Ward reflected on the best strategy for scholars in a time of repression. The opposition of authority could only be disarmed with solid research, and even under restrictions, there were still fields of research and thought where much useful work could be done. Students should follow Cardinal Newman's advice and accumulate facts rather than give vent to feelings. Ward cited St. Thomas: a tyrannical ruler must be proceeded against *non privata presumptione, sed auctoritate publica.*[24] Could not, he suggested, the gradual accumulation of the work of many scholars form a weight of opinion to be designated an *auctoritas publica?*

Ward and Pascendi

The Encyclical *Pascendi* dealt a crippling blow to the efforts of Roman

Catholics to address the issues of modernity. Its sweeping condemnation of "Modernism" grouped together in one unholy fraternity everyone outside the scholastic mold—moderate reformer and militant atheist alike. The remedy for heresy was to be rigid scholastic training, strict censorship for seminarians and clerics, and vigilance committees in every diocese.

Although his loyalty was strained to the limit, Ward never took the step of public opposition to church authorities. With other moderates, he generally took the view that public silence, instead of the support desired by the conservatives and by Rome, was the appropriate way to express dissatisfaction. However, because of his position as editor of a Catholic periodical, Ward was forced either to accept the encyclical in print or resign.

Ward viewed *Pascendi* as ultimately putting the authorities in a position that would be impossible to maintain. He conceived of his interpretation of the encyclical as a "golden bridge" that could be used to retreat from indefensible positions, and that the authorities would, if and when they faced the facts, be grateful for such an escape. A golden bridge would be better strategy than open confrontation.

> In what I shall publish anyone will be able to see that I regret much of the document. Nevertheless I think it also a duty to do what I can to prevent the ultimate effect of the part I regret from being worse than it need be and to help the authorities to recede from the appearance of taking up a position disastrous to Catholic thought.[25]

Ward's essay appeared in the January 1908 issue of the *Dublin Review*.[26] Rather than opening with the customary enthusiasm of the Catholic press for papal utterances, he made a brief statement of his duty as editor. Because authority had spoken, further discussions of the questions involved in the reconciliation of Catholic tradition and modern thought had become inappropriate for the moment, but apart from a full discussion, certain misunderstandings needed to be corrected. These concerned the impression that some doctrines taught by great theologians from Aquinas to Newman were condemned.

Ward's article was cryptic and formal. He managed to satisfy the requirements, but the task was odious to him and had pushed his integrity to the limit. He had written to his friend Willie Williams:

> I told our censor that I must resign unless I could intimate for those who read carefully that while I accept the Encyclical as a pontifical act, I do not in my own mind like it. . . . I think theological minimism a necessity. Yet

it is now getting to a point when it runs very close to sheer equivocation. . . . I believe even excessive minimism to be justifiable *under* the system while it lasts as the only way out of greater evils. Yet one should not in any way approve of the system. . . .[27]

After the article, Ward was unable to get a censor for the review. From 1908 to 1916 only two of his thirty articles concerned the reconciliation of Christianity and modern thought, and both were book reviews. He retained his editorship, but the work he had envisioned was severely curtailed.

VI. Ward's Later Reflections

For Ward, Newman provided two ways of avoiding the impossible choice between ecclesial anarchy or dictatorship: understanding the process of development in history; and having a community of Catholic scholars. In his introduction to the 1915 edition of Cardinal Newman's *On the Scope and Nature of University Education,*[28] Ward reflected on Newman's goal of a recognized body of scholars in the Catholic university that would operate as a subordinate authority or a buffer between church authorities and individual scholars.

> The guiding principle of the ruler is expediency. Such a university as Newman contemplated, on the other hand, would reach its synthesis or its practical *modus vivendi* between theology and modern research guided solely by scientific interests—theology, of course, being included among the sciences. The results thus reached would place at the disposal of Rome a body of probable conclusions which must command the respect of scholars and thoughtful men.[29]

This community would gradually produce a rational and coherent body of thought that would serve as a center of gravity for both rulers and scholars. The history of Modernism, Ward asserted, would have been widely different if Newman's ideal had been realized.

> If such a body were habitually tolerated by Roman authority, men like Loisy and Tyrrell, instead of being goaded to extremes by total lack of sympathy in authoritative quarters, might have conceivably have taken their place in the good work, . . . Such scholars, living in the society of other learned men who understood them, would not improbably have become genuinely more moderate from the presence of an opposition that was really scientific. . . . The Encyclical "Pascendi" read by itself is an eloquent witness to just that state of things I have spoken of which Newman desired to remedy, namely that Rome felt herself to be solicited by opposite extreme parties; that she felt the practical alternative to lie between sanctioning unbridled

liberty and taking measures of the utmost severity against innovation. This arose from the absence of a recognized body of discriminating thought in these complex questions.[30]

In these reflections on authority, Ward modified some of his earlier views. Wise rulers and loyal theologians did not as individuals seem to be likely to produce a *modus vivendi;* there was need for a recognized group of scholars. The tribunals in Rome were too close to the politics of authority, and the Pontifical Biblical Commission had been taken over by non-scholarly conservatives. The Catholic university seemed to offer hope for more neutral ground where the intellectual questions of the day could be aired and the authority of a consensus of Catholic scholars could be formally established.

Ward also qualified his acceptance of intellectual repression as a temporary measure necessary to protect faith in certain situations and eventually to be compensated for in the broad context of history. While he never retracted his earlier statements, in his later writing he indicated the disastrous implications of such a policy for the credibility of the church in the future.

VII. Conclusion:

Mon-archy, Syn-archy, and the Dialectic of Authority

Matthew Lamb uses the terms "mon-archy" and "syn-archy" to describe contrasting ways of dealing with a situation of pluralism.[31] The fact of pluralism in itself does not mean a fundamental relativism of values. The crucial issue is the mediation of a pluralism of values with its contradictory and complementary differences.[32] Syn-archy (pluralist cooperative [syn] principles [arche]) attempts to relate pluralism to responsible human freedom by creating, sustaining, and changing social orders through a process in which the interests of the whole community are represented, and mediating differences in ways that promote responsibility and freedom. Mon-archy (one [mon] principle [arche]) reflects an inability to relate pluralism to responsible human freedom and attempts to settle the issue of pluralism by imposing a particular set of social and cultural meanings and values through dominative power, creating, sustaining, and changing social orders through a process in which only the interests of one controlling group are represented.[33]

The rationale for the impositions of mon-archy is that there would otherwise be an-archy (no [an] principle [arche]). Together, the ideas of mon-archy and an-archy imaginatively exclude the possibility of syn-archy. This leads to a misunderstanding of the dialectics of pluralism. The real dialectic is between mon-archy/an-archy and synar-chy, not between mon-archy and an-archy, for mon-archy and an-archy are opposite sides of the assertion that pluralism and order ultimately exclude one another. [34]

Syn-archy affirms that pluralism and order include one another, but that genuine order is not imposed but mediated through the particular self-corrective processes of learning and doing of free and responsible individuals. Syn-archy means the attempt to promote these processes. It accepts human beings where they are, but does not leave them there insofar as their orientations toward intelligent truth and responsible freedom are repressed or oppressed. [35]

Ecumenical dialog provides a concrete and contemporary example of the process of syn-archy at work. At its best, it does not call upon participants to renounce deeply held convictions, but emphasizes the dynamics of dialog with others arising out of those convictions. Such dialog is not mere talk. Self-communication necessitates self-examina-tion. Self-examination in the context of the dialog generates self-critical reflection and action. It issues in calls for reform within the tradition where there have been distortions and contradictions. Such a process promotes reform, growth, change. Out of it develop affirmations of common convictions, not superimposed, but based on consensus.

Lamb's analysis of the nature and dynamics of authority indicates that the recovery of authority as cooperation and consensus is the antidote to the illusions of mon-archical dominative power, and pro-vides a general perspective for discussion and evaluation of the issue of authority in particular historical contexts.

Ward on Authority: Two Views

Ward's empirical grounding of authority had clear advantages for a more adequate self-understanding of the church in the context of mod-ern thought, and for dialog with those who would find "supernatural" legitimations problematic. Ward's recovery of the "rationality" of au-thority and tradition was valuable, in the context of his apologetics, as an antidote to the excesses of rationalism. However, the analysis of authority as representing the "reason of the race," without further qual-ification, is incomplete and neglects the complexity of authenticity and inauthenticity that comprises the concrete historical life of a tradition. The idea of a community of scholars who could temper each other's views and produce a consensus of scholarly opinion, and the need for the recognition of the authority of such a group in the modern church is also a significant, if underdeveloped, insight. Such a group would carry its own potential for authentic and inauthentic responses to the issues.

An objection to Ward's views is that his language of constitution, balance, and duty was a superimposition of categories on a clearly mon-archical structure. Contemporary critics were quick to point this out. What church, they asked, was Ward describing?[36] Further, the unverifiability of the categories was revealed by abuses of authority. There were no concrete checks and balances in Ward's scheme; it really amounted to a "gentlemen's agreement," and when the authorities did not behave in gentlemanly fashion, there was little recourse.

Looking at Ward's views on authority in the total context of his approach to apologetics, another view is possible. Ward's intention was to expand the range of imaginative possibilities beyond the unacceptable mon-archy/an-archy options. It was his style to introduce the new in the guise of a commentary on history. For him, the church retrenched against the Enlightenment as an aberration in view of a broader historical perspective. Reform would be a recovery of the principles of that wider movement. His appeal was to "the essential largeness of the capacities of Catholicism viewed historically," and he called for the abandonment of the "siege mentality" that had dominated the post–Reformation church.[37]

Ward was not hopelessly sanguine, eulogizing a nonexistent church; rather, his portrayal of the church in historical perspective was an attempt to artfully introduce an imaginative option that could become the first step toward actual change.

However one evaluates the success of Ward's particular approach and strategies, it is clear that he wrestled with the central issue. How could the principle of authority be preserved without accepting mon-archy, and the concrete reform of abuses be achieved without an-archy? Ward recognized the dilemma of mon-archy/an-archy as inadequate and envisioned the institutionalization of a syn-archical process in the Catholic university.

Imaginative Options

Ward's thought in his turn-of-the-century context is a part of the history of wrestling with the complex and critical issue of authority and order. The false dilemma of mon-archy/an-archy seems perennially to reemerge, and the development of syn-archy is ever precarious and fragile. At the root of the issue in whatever concrete historical form, is a spectrum of imaginative options. The recovery and discovery of this spectrum of options is the link between the issue in its turn of the century context and in our own. The examination and analysis of this spectrum in various historical contexts provides understanding of the dynamics and the history of wrestling with the issues of authority and order. This understanding, in turn, can be the basis for a critical perspective on the range of imaginative options in our own time and offer insights for our own efforts to wrestle with the issue of authority.

Notes

1. The summary above is based on B. Lonergan, "Dialectic of Authority," in *A Third Collection: Papers by Bernard J. P. Lonergan, S.J.*, ed. F. E. Crowe, S.J. (New York: Paulist, 1985), 5-12. Previously published in *Authority*, ed. F. J. Adelmann, S.J., Boston College Studies in Philosophy (Chestnut Hill: Boston College, 1974), 3:24-30.

2. See W. Ward, *William George Ward and the Oxford Movement* (London: Macmillan, 1893), 383-84, 390-91.

3. See "Reduced Christianity," *DR* 151 (October, 1912): 417-18, and "The Spirit of Newman's Apologetics," *New York Review* 1 (July, 1905): 3-14.

4. Reflecting on the work of Loisy, Baron Friedrich von Hügel commented: "The . . . position that our Lord himself held the proximateness of His second coming, involves the loss by churchmen of the prestige of directly divine power, since Church and Sacraments, though still the true fruits and vehicles of his life, death, and spirit, cannot thus be immediately founded by the earthly Jesus himself." See A. F. Loisy, *The Encyclopedia Britannica*, 11th ed. (Cambridge: University Press, 1911), 16:928. Quoted in Lawrence Barmann, "Friedrich von Hügel's Ideas and Activities as Modernism and as More Than Modernism," in *Modernism: Origins, Parameters, Prospects*, ed. R. Burke and G. Gilmore (Mobile: Spring Hill College Press, 1984), 67.

5. On the roots and rationale of W. G. Ward's Ultramontanism, see W. Ward, *William George Ward and the Catholic Revival* (London: Macmillan, 1893), 130-53.

6. See "R. H. Hutton as a Religious Thinker," *DR* 20 (July, 1888): 1-21.

7. See "Cardinal Newman and Constructive Religious Thought" in *Men and Matters* (London: Longmans, 1914), 47-91. First published as "Cardinal Newman and Creative Theology," *DR* 138 (April, 1906): 233-70.

8. Ibid., 376.

9. "See The Philosophy of Authority in Religion," *Hibbert Journal* 1 (July, 1903): 689.

10. The philosophers of the Enlightenment had taken their stand on individual reason in opposition to authority. In Ward's view, his contemporary, Arthur Balfour, in *Foundations of Belief* went to the other extreme. Ward offered careful corrections in a lengthy review, "The Foundations of Belief," *Quarterly*

Review 180 (April, 1895): 488-520. Republished in *Problems and Persons* (London: Longmans, 1903), 133-83.

11. Ibid., 163; see also 167-68.

12. "Philosophy of Authority," 678.

13. Ibid., 680. See also "The Exclusive Church and the Zeitgeist," the epilogue to *The Life and Times of Cardinal Wiseman* 2 vols. (London: Macmillan, 1897), 2:537-38.

14. "Authority and Reason," *American Catholic Quarterly Review* 24 (April, 1899): 171.

15. "The Exclusive Church," 537-38.

16. "Philosophy of Authority," 685.

17. Ward's source for this conception was Newman's 1877 preface to the 3rd edition of *The Via Media.*

18. "For Truth or for Life II," *DR* 140 (April, 1907): 276. See also "The Spirit of Newman's Apologetics," 9.

19. "Exclusive Church," 582. Ward cited the deposing power as an instance of this sort of variation.

20. See J. D. Root, "The Final Apostasy of St. George Jackson Mivart," *Catholic Historical Review* (January, 1985): 1-25.

21. In "Liberalism and Intransigeance," *Nineteenth Century* 47 (June, 1900): 960-73, Ward wanted to differentiate the "experts," who would reform the church, from the "extremists," who would actually prevent progress. Cited as experts were "Firmin" (Loisy), Tyrrell, and Blondel.

22. "Liberalism as a Temper of Mind," *Monthly Register* 1 (August, 1902): 177-79, and (September, 1902): 217-21.

23. "Doctores Ecclesiae," *Pilot* 3 (22 June, 1901): 774-76. Published in slightly shortened form in Maisie Ward, *Insurrection versus Resurrection* (London: Sheed & Ward, 1937), 137-41. Cited from 140.

24. "Liberalism as a Temper of Mind," 220.

25. Ward to Alfred Fawkes, 28 November 1907, *Wilfrid Ward Papers* (hereafter *WWP*), University Library, St. Andrews, Scotland, VI 12 1 (b).

26. "The Encyclical Pascendi," 142: 1-10.

27. Ward to Williams, 14 December 1907, *WWP*, VII 318a.

28. (London and New York: Everyman's Library Edition, 1915, reprint ed., 1955), vii-xxiv.

29. Ibid., xi.

30. Ibid., xii-xiii.

31. M. Lamb, "Christianity Within the Political Dialectics of Community and Empire," *Method: Journal of Lonergan Studies* 1 (Spring, 1983): 1-30. Also published in *Cities of Gods: Faith, Politics and Pluralism in Judaism, Christianity and Islam,* ed. N. Biggar (New York: Greenwood Press, 1986), 73-100.

32. Lamb, 3.

33. Dominative power is the repression of the interests and questions and the actions expressing those interests and questions of those seeking to expand effective human freedom.

34. Lamb, 11.

35. Ibid.

36. See R. E. Dell, "Mr. Wilfrid Ward's Apologetics," *Nineteenth Century* 48 (July, 1900): 127-36.

37. Introduction to *Problems and Persons*. (London: Longmans, 1903), xix. The siege mentality is described in Ward's "The Rigidity of Rome," *Nineteenth Century* 38 (December, 1895): 786-804. Republished in *Problems and Persons*, 66-98.

The Contemporary Theologian: Teacher, Prophet, Doctor

5

Brennan Hill

Department of Theology
Xavier University, Cincinnati, Ohio

O NE OF THE CENTRAL QUESTIONS in the current Roman Catholic debate over teaching authority is: By what authority do theologians teach? Since Vatican II, theologians have enjoyed a rather unique teaching authority with a considerable degree of autonomy and independence. As a result, great advances have been made in the reinterpretation and revision of the Christian tradition, and a rich pluralism has developed in the discipline.

Currently there seems to be a "restorative movement" in Rome which calls the contemporary theological movement into question. There have been censures, silencing investigations, removal of imprimaturs, suggestions of the necessity of mandates, and apparent moves to restore the Roman, neoscholastic approach to theology as normative.

This essay suggests that this conflict is, in part, the perennial tension between the charismatic and institutional functions in the church. It is further proposed that the teaching authority of theologians aptly belongs in the charismatic tradition and that this teaching authority has been repeatedly appropriated by the hierarchical offices. This does not deny the unique teaching authority of these offices, but it does assert that there is a distinct teaching charism in the church which has existed and continues to exist in its own right.

The first part of this study will deal with the nature, function, and history of the charismatic teaching authority as it existed in teachers and prophets of the early church, and as it later emerged in the highly stylized medieval garb of the university "doctor." It will be shown that in every instance this charismatic teaching authority became institutionalized in the episcopacy, in religious orders, and ultimately in the papacy. The second part will give attention to what can be retrieved and revised from these past forms of charismatic teaching to form the basis of contemporary theological authority.

I. The Teaching Charism

The "teacher" was one of the earliest charismatic figures in the early church. Paul lists the teachers as among the leaders and pioneers of the early Christian communities. "So God appointed in the church some, in the first place, as apostles; the second place, prophets; in the third place, teachers." (1 Cor 12:28) Teaching was considered to be a charismatic ministry, based on a unique gift of the Spirit, and, as Tertullian pointed out, it was not part of the church order.[1] Although the teachers apparently functioned with the approbation of the communities and their pastoral leaders, their authority was based on gift and not on delegation.[2] In communities where there was not established hierarchical authority, the teachers were called upon to resolve problems through their gifts of wisdom and knowledge. Where there were institutional leaders, the teachers had achieved such stature that the Didache had to plead with the community to give the hierarchy equal recognition.[3] Schillebeeckx points out that after the death of the "apostles and prophets," it was these teachers who became the leaders of the local communities, along with the evangelists and pastors.[4]

The early teachers spoke with such authority that their messages and decisions were accepted often without debate. The epistle of James warns its readers not to set themselves up as teachers, pointing out that there is a grave responsibility attached to their role (Jas 3:1). The author of Barnabas protests that he does not want to speak with the authority of a teacher, but rather with the much more modest voice of a brother among them (Barn 1:8 cf. 4:6). One striking story in Acts depicts Paul and Barnabas meeting with the prophets and teachers in Antioch, from where they were dutifully sent off on a missionary journey by these charismatic leaders (Acts 13:1-3).

The main function of these teachers was to pass on the Christian tradition. "Teachers were the preservers, transmitters and interpreters of tradition."[5] They were, in fact, catechists, but at a time when catechesis was seen as a central ministry in the church. They began by following up the evangelists with lucid explanations of the code, creed, and cult of the community, and later they became the central figures in the catechumenates.

The teachers also contributed to the development of the Christian tradition. As Cooke tells us, the process of "theology" appeared at the very outset, as the teachers developed new ways to clarify and interpret the Christian message.[6] This theological activity intensified as numerous "schools of theology" opened in Rome between A.D. 150 and 250. These schools of advanced study were led by the teachers, whose authority was based on their knowledge and teaching ability, not on a mandate from ecclesiastical authority.[7]

What became of this early teaching authority which played such a crucial role in establishing the early church? It would seem that this authority was appropriated by the hierarchical offices in the church. As the episcopacy and the presbyterate became more universal in the second and third centuries, the unique and independent charism so characteristic of the teacher all but disappeared. Schoonenberg points out that concern over Gnostic extremes in teaching and other heresies moved the bishops to take on the teaching authority in order to defend the faith. In addition, many of the hierarchical leaders did not have enough confidence in the laity to allow them to carry on the teaching function.[8] After Nicea, public theology was not usually carried out by lay people, but by bishops, such as Athanasius and Augustine. The pastoral and teaching functions had become joined in the hierarchy.

II. The Prophetic Charism

As was already noted, the prophets are listed in the New Testament among the early charisms. Paul includes them in his list in 1 Corinthians, and in Ephesians the prophets are described as the very foundation of the church (Eph 2:20). Ruef interprets this to mean that the prophets were both leaders and lawmakers in the early Christian communities.[9]

As in the case of the teachers, the prophets spoke with an extraordinary authority. The *Didache* says that once the prophet's word is authenticated by the way the prophet lives, that word must go unchallenged. The prophet was a teacher and more, because the prophets experienced unique movements of the Spirit. Barclay observes that they were not "fore-tellers," as commonly thought, but "forth-tellers" of the word of God, a word that apparently had a unique and profound effect on them.[10] They had been gifted with such a unique encounter with the Holy, that they were compelled to share their inspiration with others. They spoke as people whose teaching and lives were possessed by the Holy Spirit.[11]

The prophets not only understood the Christian message profoundly, they were able to apply the message to particular circumstances, thus making the will of the risen Lord known to the community. Käsemann claims that many of the prophets were wandering teachers, who were able to address local faith problems through admonitions, warnings, judgments and consolations.[12] Related to their charism was their ability to perceive the nature of life situations and to apply the teachings of Jesus to these situations. They were able to link the word with life, the human with the divine. As Heschel puts it, the prophet's "true greatness is his ability to hold God and man in a single thought."[13]

This is done, not as is so commonly thought in an atmosphere of judgment, but rather in one of reconciliation. Attendant to the prophet's ability to relate the message to life, was the prophet's ability to spot inconsistencies. When the prophets perceived ways of living that were not consistent with the gospel, they gave exhortations and provocations, rather than instructions. This, according to Gryson, gave the prophet a more spectacular character than the teacher.[14] Confrontation was often a part of the prophetic ministry. In both Testaments, the prophets challenged distortions in doctrine, injustices, misuse of authority, acts of violence, and abuses of human dignity. The prophets declared all such abuses to be incompatible with the holy will of the saving God. Brueggeman sums it up this way: "Prophetic ministry consists of offering an alternative perception of reality and in letting people see their history in the light of God's freedom and his will for justice."[15]

The prophet's call is a call for reform, not only in society, but in the religious tradition itself. Deeply rooted in the tradition, the prophets constantly called for a return to the uncorrupted substance of the tradition. At the same time, they often called for a reinterpretation of the tradition, lest it atrophy.[16] Obviously this persistent urging for reform and renewal at times put the prophets in positions of dissent from the established authority.

Prophets were also concerned with the future. As von Rad points out, this does not mean that they foretold the future as popular belief would have it. Rather, they were able to envision the future of the people of God in terms of what would be possible for them if they followed God's word.[17] They were messengers of hope and potential, encouraging their people to reach beyond the limitations of the now. They could perceive the beginnings of the actions of God in history and could alert their people to the fresh possibilities ahead. Concomitantly, they could sense dangerous futures which were being formulated by present actions and decisions.

What happened to this prophetic charism? It would seem that, as in the case of the teaching charism, it all but disappeared as a unique and identifiable ministry toward the end of the third century. This charism also was absorbed into the institutional structures, appearing at times at some of the great bishops, or in members of the emerging monastic orders. As Cooke observes, this resulted in an unfortunate institutionalization of a key charism, and prevented those outside the structures from speaking with an authoritative prophetic voice.[18]

III. The Medieval Doctor

We have seen how the charismatic ministries of teacher and prophet were absorbed into institutional offices in the course of the third century. Gryson tells us that it would be a long time before such unique teaching authority would appear again. "We must wait ten centuries before the reappearance in the church of a teaching function endowed with a real autonomy and invested with a proper authority, one which was not merely delegated by the ecclesiastical hierarchy. We must await the advent of the medieval universities."[19] This teaching function came in the form of the medieval "doctor."

In the form of the doctor, the teaching charism is described in terms that are distinctively medieval. Schoonenberg describes the perspective: "The society that grows out of the feudal system, is ideologically supported by a vision in which all of God's gifts descend along higher and lower grades of being."[20] Each person's position in a hierarchical society was determined by function, whether it be combat, prayer, commerce, or in the case of the doctor, scholarship. The doctors were those who searched for truth, scholars who were gifted with a special supernatural light which enabled them to give ultimate sense to life and to guide human beings to God.[21]

The medieval doctors did not use their theological charism to be catechists or apologists, as did the earlier teachers. Rather, the doctors functioned as judges of orthodoxy. St. Thomas held that the foremost duty of the Christian doctor was the protection of doctrinal purity and the pursuit and refutation of heresies.[22] For the most part the medieval bishops left it to the theologians to decide on doctrinal matters. In the case of heresy, it was the theologian who made the decision on orthodoxy, and it was the bishop who decreed condemnation or even burning at the stake. In fact, it was the decisions of theologians that put to death the Grand Master of the Knights Templar, Joan of Arc, and Jon Hus. As Schoonenberg wryly remarks, theologians who today demand the recognition of their human rights from the hierarchy, must remember that their own history is far from spotless.[23]

The doctors belonged to an exclusive guild called the "university," where they presided over their student apprentices. Once achieving the doctorate, the theologian was authorized as worthy of teaching authority, and could teach as a qualified witness of the faith. He was part of a triumverate of power: the *Regnum;* the *Sacerdotium;* and the *Studium.* Just as the sovereignty of God was mediated through the king, and salvation mediated through the priest, revelation was mediated through the doctor.[24]

These medieval doctors enjoyed tremendous prestige and many privileges. They were exempt from taxes, arrest, and punishment by torture. Those who were members of the clergy had extra exemptions and found it easy to obtain benefices. In the medieval society, the doctors held the same dignity as the episcopate. Their title was the equivalent to that of nobility.[25] In the universities, the doctors held more prestige than their colleagues in the other sciences because theology was "the queen of the sciences." It was considered that theology gave ultimate meaning to the other sciences and was the very center of the university structure. Those who taught this discipline could even anticipate a higher reward in heaven!

As in the early church, theologians enjoyed a unique autonomy and did not view themselves subject to the hierarchy. Bishops and theologians were not usually seen to be in competition, because they exercised two different kinds of authority, the authority of the "pastoral chair" and the authority of the "professional chair." Both authorities seemed to be on the same footing. Congar cites several instances of conflict, such as when Gregory IX wrote the University of Paris in 1231, warning about the use of Aristotelian philosophy, and Bishop Templer's condemnation of the work of Albert the Great and St. Thomas. Neither complaint seemed to have much effect. In fact, fifty years after Templer's condemnation, Thomas was canonized.[26] One important reason why the bishops did not challenge the authority of the theologians was that many of the hierarchy came from the nobility and did not have the training to meddle in theological affairs. If there were any conflicts, most of them were between contending theological schools. When one opponent appealed to the Holy See to condemn the other, the denunciations were not taken very seriously. The doctors usually claimed to be merely "proposing," not "affirming," and were thus excused of heresy. The Inquisition itself was set up to combat heresy among the people, not among the doctors.[27]

The authority of the theologians eventually went beyond scholarship. They spoke and even voted on councils, censured errors without consulting the pastoral leaders, and even challenged hierarchical decrees. By the time of the Great Schism of the West, the bishops were in such a state of decadence, that the theologians were literally in charge of doctrine. This reached a climax at the General Councils of Basel and Constance in the fifteenth century, where only a handful of bishops were present amidst hundreds of theologians.[28]

This dominance of the theologians was not to last. Schoonenberg points out that even before Trent, the hierarchy around the pope took control and began to consider doctrinal matters under their authority.[29] Yet, many of the doctors maintained their authority throughout the Reformation, participating in the condemnation of Luther and making major contributions at the Council of Trent. This authority gradually weakened and finally gave way in the wake of the French Revolution, and in Napoleon's closings of the centers of theological authority, the universities. Even though the term "magisterium" was still attached to the theologians during the nineteenth century, they played a subordinate role in the church's teaching authority. Their chief function became to set forth and defend the teaching of the papacy and the episcopacy.[30]

Teaching authority was henceforth seen as part of the juridical authority. Schillebeeckx sums up the situation as follows:

> The magisterium became very doctrinaire regarding the theologians who were thought to have no teaching authority other than that doled out to them by reason of a "canonical mission." It was a time of all sorts of "mandates" and "canonical missions" and the dominant image of the church was one in which every gift from above came to the church through the pope.[31]

The charism of teaching had once again been institutionalized, now in even a more narrow sense than before, since it was confined primarily to the papacy. This situation prevailed until the Second Vatican Council, which restored the collegial teaching authority of the bishops and once again recognized the expertise of theologians, allowing them to collaborate in the formulation of the documents.

IV. The Sorting Out Process

As already noted, the charismatic teaching authority has been carried out in three unique roles in the history of the church. Each of these roles, teacher, prophet, and doctor, was shaped by the culture and the needs of the Christian community of a given period. Much of what we have seen can be by-passed as no longer relevant to the expression of the charism. The theologian today does not have the unquestionable authority or the power of leadership that was exercised by the early teachers. Neither do theologians now enjoy the unchallenged authority or juridical power of the early prophets. And, most certainly, today's scholars do not have the prestigious social standing or unique autonomy that belonged to the medieval doctors. But the charism is still evident in that the theologian is today recognized as a uniquely gifted person, called to teach, to take prophetic stands, and to work as a responsible academic in the service of the ecclesial community.

In the next section we discuss the elements of these past ministries which can be seen in continuity with the exercise of theology today. We will begin by examining three areas wherein today's theologian stands in continuity with the early teachers of the church: (1) gifted ministry, (2) catechesis, and (3) development of the tradition.

A Gifted Ministry

As in the case of the teachers of the early church, the contemporary theologian exercises a charismatic ministry. Ministry has been defined as "a public action by Christians for their church as service of the Kingdom of God."[32] If such a definition is acceptable, "doing theology" indeed qualifies as a ministry. The theologian as writer, teacher, or consultant publicly serves the Christian community in a unique fashion. As a person who has spent years studying, interpreting, and communicating the Christian message, the theologian can competently assist others in understanding and living the gospel.

The basic foundation of this teaching charism is the gift of faith. As Dulles writes: "The work of the theologian has an ecclesial foundation in that the theologian is baptized, a believing member of the church."[33] Naturally, this gift of faith is individualized in each person and combined with that person's unique capabilities to serve as a teacher. Charism is always a combination of divine gift and human capability. As O'Meara puts it: "The human and divine forces which confirm a Christian in a special ministry . . . draw on the ontic and charismatic structure given to the personality by birth as well as by baptism."[34]

Besides faith and personal abilities, the theologian must exhibit an extraordinary grasp of the Christian tradition. Like the early teachers, the theologian's authority will only be accepted if the community discerns such understanding. As Cooke points out: "The only ground for legitimate authority in teaching is accurate understanding. One communicates truth only if one possesses truth. Truth cannot be legislated, even by one who has the highest legitimate authority in the church; truth must be discovered."[35] As with the early teachers, a deep understanding of the Christian tradition is integral to the present exercise of the charism of theology.

Catechesis

As we have seen, the early teachers served as catechists. Today many theologians would shy away from viewing themselves in this role, because it often implies nonprofessional volunteers who work largely with children in pastoral programs. Such separation of theology and catechesis is unfortunate. This is not to deny that these are two separate and distinct ministries. At the same time, they are both closely related, in that catechists must understand theology, and that there is a catechetical dimension to the theologian's work. Both are ministries of the word, and each is concerned with nurturing faith.[36]

Faith is indeed at the very heart of the theologian's work. Whether we define theology in classical Anselmian terms as "faith seeking understanding," or in the modern Rahnerian sense of "the conscious and methodical explanation of the divine revelation received and grasped in faith," the center of the whole enterprise is faith.[37] The theologian-teacher is constantly dealing with faith, in interpreting its content, its application, or its need for nurturing in the lives of students.

Serving these faith needs of students does not imply imposing or imparting faith. As Rahner has observed, faith is never awakened by bringing something from outside the person. Rather, faith involves "an understanding of what has already been experienced in the depth of human reality as grace."[38] As teacher, the theologian operates within an already existing ambience of faith, and influences faith in the very process of theologizing. Theology is, in fact, a way of exercising faith, a process which by its very nature can deepen faith. Schoonenberg puts it splendidly:

Theology is a distinct way of practicing the faith; it is faith in the form of reflection. Theology is faith responding to the message it may receive as it turns in contemplation, both to God who addresses us and to the world to which God's message is addressed.[39]

The theologian need only attend to good teaching, and this alone could have a positive effect on students' faith development.

This catechetical dimension of theology has produced considerable debate in departments of theology. Some feel that such departments should focus on religious education and attempt to compensate for inadequate religious formation on the part of students. Others object that this would be to engage in "higher catechesis," an endeavor unworthy of an academic department.[40] Then there is the protest that theology is itself too denominational, too controlled by ecclesiastical authority to be considered a genuine academic subject. They would admit theology into the curriculum only if it is subject to the demands of public criteria, namely evidence, critique, and disciplined evaluation.[41] As a result, there is a trend to opt for "religious studies" rather than theology, in order to ensure scientific objectivity and to avoid the issue of faith commitment on the part of students and teachers.

There are sound arguments for maintaining strong theological commitments on campuses, especially those that are church-affiliated. This does not mean that the theologian is concerned with indoctrination, winning converts, or training apologists. None of these activities would be compatible with genuine academic education. At the same time, theologians are concerned with the faith needs of their students. These needs, of course, vary widely. Some students are alienated from religion, others are on "leave of absence" from organized religions, some are searching for faith. Then there are students who have a strong faith commitment and are looking for deeper understanding and nourishment. There is no reason why the theologian cannot be academically respectable and yet serve this variety of needs. To all, the theologian can offer clear understanding, relevant interpretation, and options that are intelligently conceived.

Development of the Tradition

The Christian tradition is not a rigid deposit moving through time in unchangeable formulas. It is a dynamic, living tradition, which has been continually reinterpreted for each age and culture. Biblical scholar George MacRae, whose untimely death recently saddened all of us, wrote:

> One might say that it is a consequence of the doctrine of the incarnation that God can be portrayed taking the risk of revealing himself in the human.

> If all the utterances by which revelation is communicated to us are utterances
> in human language, that is, as is often said, "God speaks to us in the language
> of humanity," then we must interpret God's speech as we interpret the
> language of humanity.[42]

Interpretation and development of the tradition are at the heart of the
theologian's work. Whether it be an Augustine interpreting the need
for grace in the fifth century, an Aquinas explaining the power of God
for the medieval church, a Rahner giving the twentieth century a new
vision of church, or a Schüssler Fiorenza offering a feminine reconstruction of tradition, the theologian plays a key role in the development
of the Christian message.

John XXIII, in his now classical statement at the opening of Vatican
II, said that while the church must remain faithful to the sacred patri-
mony of truth received from the Fathers, it must look to the present,
to new conditions in the modern world. The substance of the message
will remain the same, but the forms will change. This notion was later
incorporated into the Vatican Council's Document on Revelation,
which recognized the development of doctrine and the contribution
of theologians, as well as it recognized the teaching authority of the
hierarchy.

> This tradition which comes from the apostles develops in the church with
> the help of the Holy Spirit. For there is a growth in the understanding of
> the realities and words which have been handed down. This happens through
> the contemplation and study made by believers . . . and through the preaching
> of those who have received through episcopal succession the sure gift of
> truth.[43]

The hermeneutical enterprise is as much the responsibility of theologians today as it was for the first teachers in the early schools of theology.

V. The Prophetic Dimension of Theology

Peace and justice issues, such as the nuclear arms race and economic
injustice, as well as the critical areas of oppression by liberation theology,
have once again brought into focus the prophetic dimension of theology.
The contemporary theologian might well be seen in continuity with
the gifted prophet of early Christianity. In this next section we will
examine three functions of the prophetic spirit which link the theologian today with this ancient charism: (1) application of the message,
(2) the exercise of critique, and (3) the suggestion of futures.

The Application of the Message

The early Christian prophets were, in part, teachers; they spoke as "ones who knew" the message intellectually as well as experientially. But they were more than teachers; they were also gifted with the ability to apply the Christian message to particular situations and problems. In today's church one thinks of the great moralists, like Häring and so many others, who revolutionized moral theology and who have given us new methods for applying gospel values to the extremely complex ethical issues of today. We recognize the work of Murray as helping us understand how the gospel applies to the contemporary problems of religious freedom and the relation of church and state. We acknowledge the courageous work of Schillebeeckx in addressing the critical problem of ministry in today's church, and Radford Ruether's contribution to the Jewish-Christian dialogue. We think of Gutiérrez, and the many other liberation theologians who have taught us to listen to the poor and the oppressed to discover deeper meanings of human dignity, the Christ, and church. They have taught us how to apply the teachings of Jesus to the resistance of violence and injustice. These and many other contemporary theologians have shown us how the charism of prophecy is still quite operative in today's church.

This prophetic application of the Christian message to particular circumstances is especially appropriate in today's classrooms. Today's students expect the application of the tradition to their everyday lives. They express confusion, doubt, and a need to search, which requires the teacher not only to interpret the gospel, but also to show how it might relate to their immediate questions and problems. This does not imply a need for "trendy theology" or some sort of forced relevance. It does suggest that theologians avoid the needless jargon and esoteric speculation which can alienate students from theology. Somehow theology must be prophetic in the sense that it gives students insights and experiences which they can take into their careers, and into their personal and family lives. Unless theology can speak to the here and now, it will be at best a curiosity and at worst a bore.

The Exercise of Critique

The early Christian prophets had the ability to see inconsistencies between the message and the way it was being lived. Today's theologian might describe this activity more in terms of "critique." As Tracy has pointed out, the theologian today addresses three audiences and exercises a critical function toward each of them.[44]

Toward the first audience, the public culture, the theologian is ambivalent. On the one hand, theology looks at the world much more positively than it did in the past. The advances in the modern disciplines are not only recognized, but also are used as the very tool for studying the Christian tradition. Moreover, the theologian lives in a church that describes itself as a servant to the modern world, in that it has a mission to preach Christ's transforming message to the world. Positive contributions of a world that is now secular, such as human development, technological advances, political liberation, democratic procedures, and assistance to the needy and oppressed are recognized and supported. The theologian is thus engaged in signaling the saving power of God within the world as well as within organized religion. The prophetic function here is in assisting people to recognize these signs and in helping Christians foster such positive movements within culture. As Häring puts it:

> The more Christians respect the relative autonomy of the various realms of life . . . the more will they be able to fulfill their prophetic role. That role is to integrate carefully all that is good, true, beautiful and noble, to eliminate everything that contradicts faith, to purify whatever is in need of purification.[45]

The other side of the prophetic is the recognition of the dark side of culture and human experience. Increasingly we hear theology challenging systemic sin in society, addressing issues like militarism, sexism, prejudice, and social oppression. From those more radical, we even hear of theologians who are called to identify more closely with the poor and with the church that is being born from their midst. "The prophetic experience is an experience of one's own powerlessness in the experience of the power of God; and there is always the experience of God's holiness and mercy in a total solidarity with the suffering, the downtrodden, the poor."[46]

The theologian also exercises critique toward a second audience, the church. Positively, this means that the theologian has the responsibility to interpret carefully the church's tradition, and to represent fairly what the contemporary church teaches. Prophetic theology ensures that the church has a right to speak for Christ on issues of morality, peace, and justice. Prophetic theology struggles against a privatized notion of church which keeps religion and world separated. Given the high visibility that the church has today in so many moral and social issues, the theologian should have ample opportunity to take such a prophetic stance.

A more delicate issue is the role of the theologian in critiquing injustices in the church itself and in dissenting from official church positions. Obviously, theology, if it is to be academically credible, must honestly and responsibly critique whatever prejudice, injustice, or abuses of freedom are observed in the church itself. As for dissent, the possibility for responsible dissent from the noninfallible teaching authority in the church would seem to be integral to any learned person's approach to an issue.[47]

Finally, the prophetic dimension of theology concerns the academy itself. Schoonenberg has pointed out the need for the academy to do more critiquing of what goes on in its own house. He writes:

> Especially theologians with such particular approaches as political, liberation, feminist, and black theology intend to be critical prophets; the theological community as a whole, however, must meet these critical prophets with its own metacriticism.[48]

It is unfortunate that so often this critical function of the academy is taken over by official ecclesiastical authorities. As a result, the atmosphere of openness that should surround scholarly work is stifled by apprehension and even fear. This is hardly conducive to creative and productive research. Moreover, such an atmosphere might in itself prevent members of the academy from critiquing a colleague, lest such criticism invite official scrutiny.

The Suggestion of Futures

The early prophets were "forth-tellers" in that they proclaimed the word, projecting hopeful futures if the word is heard, and warning of disastrous futures for those opposing the kingdom. Theologians today play a similar role. On the hopeful side, one thinks of Teilhard and his vision of evolution moving toward its fulfillment in Christ, or of Moltmann and his "theology of hope." In a more foreboding vein, one thinks of the warnings of theologians and bishops regarding the dangers of nuclear war, or of the potential for violence and bloodshed in South Africa if social justice is not established there.

Theology is not properly done in isolation today. It is done within a world which stands perilously close to its own destruction. It is responsible for bringing to that world the message which challenges the injustice and violence that lies beneath this peril. The prophetic dimension of theology is not negotiable in our times.

VI. The Doctor Today

Questions about academic freedom, mandates, and the ecclesiastical control of Catholic universities have caused a great deal of discussion about the identity of the theologian in higher education. In this section, we will suggest what might be retrieved from the medieval doctorate and incorporated into the function of the modern-day academic. We will look at two aspects of the doctorate: (1) scholarship and (2) autonomy.

Scholarship

The theologian does not enjoy the privileged and prestigious position of the medieval doctor, but does continue the doctoral tradition of being a professional scholar. Of course, theology is no longer viewed as "queen of the sciences," nor is it at the center of the curriculum. Theology is an academic discipline alongside many other disciplines and is subject to the same public expectations of careful research, credible evidence, and clear presentations. The theologian in an institution of higher education is expected to be a master of a field—whether it be moral theology, biblical studies, systematic or historical theology—and a well-qualified researcher and educator. No quarter is given because of the religious nature of the discipline, and the theologian is evaluated by students, departments, administrators and tenure committees, just as is any other professor. A rather wide array of gifts and talents is required of the theologian who is to survive in today's academic competition.

Even though theology is classified as a standard discipline, it has a unique characteristic. It is the only discipline in the academic institution that is also responsible to another community, namely the church, both communal and institutional. The theologian represents an ecclesiastical tradition that is confessional by nature. Orthodoxy, as it was in the medieval university, is always a factor, and even in the free and open atmosphere of a college or university there is a serious responsibility regarding doctrine. This entails a fair representation of the official views of the church, as well as a presentation of varying and even dissenting views. Theology cannot be considered a valid academic subject unless all credible interpretations of the Christian tradition are studied and discussed in an atmosphere of openness and freedom. At the same time, the theologian must be sensitive to the "*sensus fidelium*" and must educate in a "dialogue of fellowship," rather than in a framework of religious indoctrination. All of this puts tremendous demands upon the theologian who is expected to be well informed, intellectually honest, and yet loyal to the task of helping "the church always deepen her knowledge of the mystery of Christ."[49]

Autonomy

The autonomy of the theologian is a crucial issue in today's church. Clearly much of the autonomy that the teaching charism enjoyed in the past was culturally conditioned. When past teachers and prophets carried on their ministry, the hierarchical offices were not as established as they are today. The doctors taught at a time when many of the bishops were not concerned about doctrinal matters. Today's picture is quite different. The teaching authority of the church is now broadly based, and includes papal authority, episcopal authority, the teaching authority of the Council, the Synod, the Episcopal conference, the authority of the faithful, as well as theological authority. With such a complicated network of teaching authority, it is no wonder that there is tension and that the theologian at times feels like an embattled witness.

Previous to Vatican II, many theologians considered that their teaching authority was delegated and that they were in fact merely sharing in the authority of the Roman magisterium functioning largely as couriers for the Holy See. Theologians who were doing original research and proposing alternative views were considered to be marginal, or perhaps dangerous.

The Vatican Council radically changed the image of theologians. They were recognized as having a unique authority in their own right; they worked closely with the hierarchy in formulating the documents of the Council. The whole process was a marvelous example of "shared authority," with the charismatic teaching authority working closely with the papal and episcopal teaching authority. Theology was never the same after that. From then on it was carried out as an exact science, dealing honestly with historical, exegetical, and interpretative data. Theology would make use of other disciplines heretofore held suspect, and would become pluralistic, ecumenical, liberational, and from below as well as from above. It is no small wonder that church administrators, who have the task of keeping some semblance of order in the house, became increasingly concerned.

If ecclesiastical authority moves beyond concern toward overt interference and obstruction, it will be most difficult to exercise the charism of theology effectively. Perhaps some suggestions are in order. First, both those in official and academic authority need to realize that they are subject to the authority of the Spirit and the gospel. Second, a mutual respect of the hierarchical teaching authority, and what might be termed the charismatic teaching authority, is called for. Both play a role in the church's enterprise of preserving and interpreting the Christian tradition. As Avery Dulles says, both authorities are "complementary and mutually corrective."[50] Each must have adequate autonomy to carry out properly its respective task.

VII. A Composite of a Charism

The teaching charism, as it was exercised by the teacher, prophet, and doctor, is today uniquely exercised by the contemporary theologian. This charism might be described as a gifted ministry that nourishes faith and contributes to the development of the Christian tradition. It is prophetic in that it gives application of the tradition, provides critique and confrontation, and offers a future, both hopeful and foreboding. It is a charism which often operates in an academic setting where it exercises scholarship with a unique autonomy. Schoonenberg sums it up well when he writes: "It is precisely the teacher, sometimes speaking prophetically, but usually imparting ordered wisdom and knowledge, who most clearly embodies an historical beginning for what theologians are now."[51]

In Sullivan's fine work on the teaching authority of the church, he reminds us that a charism is a gift of grace, a genuine gift that can be discerned as the work of the Holy Spirit. The thesis of this essay would agree with his position that there is a vocation to do theology as an ecclesial ministry. Those who have the gifts, and who conscientiously cultivate these gifts, should be free to devote themselves "generously and fruitfully to the service of the Word of God and his people."[52]

Notes

1. R. Gryson, "The Authority of the Teacher in the Ancient and Medieval Church," *JES* 19 (1982): 177.

2. B. Cooke, *Ministry to Word and Sacraments* (Philadelphia: Fortress, 1976), 63.

3. Gryson, 177.

4. E. Schillebeeckx, Ministry: *Leadership in the Community of Jesus* (New York: Crossroad, 1981), 13.

5. J. Ruef, *Paul's First Letter to the Corinthians* (Philadelphia: Westminster, 1977), 138.

6. Cooke, 225.

7. Gryson, 178. Cf. G. Brady, "Les écoles romaines au second siècle," *RHE* 28 (1982): 501-32.

8. P. Schoonenberg, "The Theologian's Calling, Freedom and Constraint," *JES* 19 (1982): 97-98.

9. Ruef, 138.

10. W. Barclay, *The Letters to the Corinthians* (Philadelphia: Westminster, 1975), 111.

11. J. Jeremias, *New Testament Theology* (New York: Harper & Row, 1971), 78.

12. E. Käsemann, *Commentary on Romans* (Grand Rapids: Eerdmans, 1980), 340 and 354.

13. A. Heschel, *The Prophets* (New York: Harper & Row, 1962), 20.

14. Gryson, 176.

15. W. Brueggemann, *The Prophetic Imagination* (Philadelphia: Fortress, 1976), 110.

16. G. von Rad, *The Message of the Prophets* (New York: Harper & Row, 1965), 110.

17. Ibid.

18. Cooke, 244.

19. Gryson, 182.

20. Schoonenberg, 98.

21. Gryson, 21.

22. Y. Congar, *A History of Theology* (New York: Doubleday and Co., 1968), 113.

23. Schoonenberg, 99.

24. Ibid., 98.

25. Gryson, 187.

26. Congar, 113.

27. Y. Congar, "The Magisterium and the Theologians—A Short History," *TD* 25 (1977): 17.

28. Ibid., 18.

29. Schoonenberg, 99.

30. Congar, "The Magisterium," 18.

31. E. Schillebeeckx, "The Magisterium and Ideology," *JES* 19 (1982): 16.

32. T. O'Meara, *Theology of Ministry* (New York: Paulist, 1983), 176.

33. A. Dulles, "The Two Magisteria: An Interim Reflection," *CTSA Proceedings* 35 (1980): 159.

34. O'Meara, 178.

35. B. Cooke, "The Responsibility of Theologians," *Commonweal* 39 (1980): 41.

36. *Theologians and Catechists in Dialogue,* ed. B. Hill and M. R. Newland (Dubuque: Wm. C. Brown Co., 1977).

37. K. Rahner, "Theology," *Sacramentum Mundi VI* (New York: Herder & Herder, 1970), 234.

38. Ibid., II, 311.

39. Schoonenberg, 94. Cf. his essay, "Theologie als Kritische Prophetie," in *Die Funktion der Theologie in Kirche und Gesellschaft*, ed. P. Neuenzeit (Munich: Kösel Verlag, 1969), 371-85.

40. L. J. O'Connell, "Religious Studies, Theology and the Humanities Curriculum," *JAAR* 52 (1984): 731-37.

41. D. Tracy, *The Analogical Imagination* (New York: Crossroad, 1981), 21 ff.

42. G. MacRae, "The Gospel and the Church," *TD* 24 (1976): 338-48.

43. *The Documents of Vatican II*, ed. Walter M. Abbott, S.J. (New York: Herder & Herder, 1966), 116.

44. Tracy, 29f (f.).

45. B. Häring, *Free and Faithful in Christ III*, (New York: Crossroad, 1981), 150.

46. Ibid., 137.

47. F. A. Sullivan, *Magisterium: Teaching Authority in the Catholic Church* (New York: Paulist, 1983), 166-71.

48. Schoonenberg, "The Theologian's Calling," 94.

49. Pope John Paul II, "Papal Address to International Theological Commission," *Origins* 9 (1979): 394.

50. A. Dulles, "The Theologian," 235-46.

51. Schoonenberg, "The Theologian's Calling," 243.

52. Sullivan, 201.

Part 2

Part 2

Theology and Authority: An Anthropological Analysis

6

Leland J. White

Department of Theology
St. John's University

T HEOLOGY AND AUTHORITY: what do these terms mean to Americans? To Vatican bureaucrats? What did they mean to medieval theologians? Do the Hebrew scriptures or the New Testament have equivalent terms? "Theology" and "authority" must be understood within the varying historical contexts of those who speak of them.

"God," "humans," and "nature" challenge historical imagination because the meaning of such terms is commonly tacitly understood rather than explicitly defined in documents available to historians. Sometimes even historians naively assume that tacit understandings from their own world apply in other cultures. When they are more critical, they may rely on texts available to their historical subjects to define these terms. In any case, historians have limited resources for dealing with tacit meanings.

Cultural anthropologists, on the other hand, have tested a number of methods for uncovering the tacit understandings in social life. These social science research models are designed to probe the range and variability of human motivation. From this perspective, theology is not seen primarily as a system of ideas in which the idea of authority might play a part. Instead, "theology," "authority," and yes, even "God" are seen as symbols whose meaning is to be assessed from the way they appear to function in social life. Verbal symbols and symbolic actions alike—"love" or the act of kissing—are interpreted in terms of how they are used. Anthropologists assume that "theology" and "authority" embody and refer to activities, actors, and interactions within particular social settings.[1] At least part of what is latently understood when these terms are used is their socially constructed meaning.

I. The Social Construction of "Theology"

To say "theology" is a social construction means that what passes for "theology" is created by individuals who are recognized as theologians, who teach in collaboration with colleagues in departments of religion, religious studies, or theology, and who submit their research to peer review in professional journals and seminars.[2] In the same way, "literature" is also a social construction.[3]

Socially constructed realities require legitimation. To be assured that what they are doing is indeed "theology," theologians employ norms. These include professional standards, customary procedures, and rules of theological discourse. Measured by these norms, which are themselves social constructs, theological statements become authoritative or valid.

On the one hand, more traditional theologians would choose to speak of the *authority* of statements that measure up to their norms. Likewise they may measure their own statements against theological statements they consider authoritative. In some cases authoritative judges, e.g. the ecclesiastical magisterium, might measure their "orthodoxy" or "heresy." On the other hand, many contemporary theologians might choose not to speak of authority, but rather to speak of other types of validity such as *probability* or *meaningfulness*. In these instances, the measure takes greater account of the interactive relationships between the theological statement and other realities.

In whatever way theologians might speak, they need to know where their norms come from, to know not only whether particular theological statements are legitimate, but even to know what these statements mean. Words and norms have meanings in particular cultural settings. For example, take the word *quickest*: our minds plot the *quickest* route from New York to San Francisco in different ways, depending on whether we think in terms of trailways, highways, sea lanes, or air routes. The person who proposes such a trip assumes that "everybody knows" that humans travel across land or sea as though on a flat surface, or that they may travel in the air perhaps "as the crow flies," i.e. across the flat surface, or in an arc across the pole, thereby recognizing the surface covered as spherical rather than flat.

Likewise, in one cultural setting, conversation requires a proximity that brings individuals face to face. In another setting, physical manipulation of air waves allows us to converse with no more than an exchange of sounds. To know what "speaking with" means is to know the range of social interactions to which it might be referred. The range of social interactions, seldom explicitly described, is assumed by members of any given social group. To understand members of other groups with which we share little or no common life, we have to know how they interact among themselves. We need to know the world from which their words come.

II. Interpretation Relies on Cultural Scripts

Other worlds can be reconstructed by careful study of the words them-selves, one by one. Research of this kind is helpful, but slow. None of us learned either the meanings of our own words or the rules by which we connected them one by one. From infancy we grasped rather large blocks of meaningful statements. From these large blocks, we inferred the meaning of individual terms and the rules for relating one term to another, as well as how all these things related to our own life experi-ence. We picked up words and meanings, as they appeared in episodic references and stories. We became familiar with patterns in all of this, and learned to anticipate meanings because of the patterns. We came to know certain plots and to recognize certain cues so well that we can readily infer plots that were seldom mentioned. In short, we have learned scripts and became skilled in contextualizing the utterances of others within our culture in a multiplicity of familiar scripts.

To understand people in other cultures we must also learn their scripts. We study other languages and literature as well as history. We know the differences between translating and understanding others' stories. Nonetheless, we often translate the particulars of others' stories, interpreting the particulars within our own familiar scripts, as the more naive historians already mentioned sometimes do. Thus, the Hebrew *Yahweh* becomes the Latin *Dominus* or the English *Lord,* as though a tribal Protector, a universal Overlord and a personal Savior were the same.

Different cultural scripts have assigned different roles to God as well as humans. Translating word for word, we inevitably misinterpret others' meanings. Worse, we may misconstrue why they found it meaningful, because the norms underlying a script are generally less explicit than the plot. Fundamental norms, precisely because they are accepted within a given social world, are likely to be tacit.

To study cultural scripts and the norms governing meaning within them becomes ever more complex. In New Testament courses, I must acquaint undergraduate Americans with a first-century text written by Greco-Roman Jews. My students have already heard it proclaimed liturgically by twentieth-century pastors, who may have studied bits and pieces of the text in the systematic statements of European theologians. To perceive all these layers of meaning might be enriching, but to avoid reducing all the layers of meaning to the range of meaning afforded by more familiar scripts is a challenge.

III. A Cross-cultural Model

Are there cross-cultural patterns in the endless number of scripts people use? Are there patterns that will allow us to ask some of the right questions when we confront material from any cultural tradition? Are there questions that will help us anticipate the probable master scripts behind any statement? A task force of the Catholic Biblical Association chaired by Bruce Malina has given considerable attention to fundamental cultural patterns suggested by anthropologist Mary Douglas.[4] The Douglas model analyzes and compares cultures in terms of two variables, which yield four fundamental patterns.

Douglas's first variable is "group." How much pressure is exerted on the individual or subgroup to conform to the demands of the larger social group? How intense is the sense of "we," of lines marking group boundaries? Social interactions, and hence meanings, are shaped by whether the sense of "group" is strong or weak and how strong or how weak.

The second variable is "grid." How do socially shared conceptions square with individual or group experience in everyday life? Social interactions and meanings are colored by the expectation that life will confirm one's values (high grid) or disconfirm one's values (low grid).

If we graph the two variables on a cross-bar, representing positive and negative degrees of group and grid, we find four fundamental cultural patterns, strong-group/high-grid, strong-group/low-grid, weak-group/high-grid and weak-group/low-grid (see Figure A).

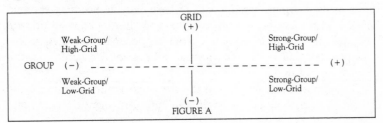

FIGURE A

These four rather abstract patterns allow us to ask the same questions about any script that might stand behind any statement, whether of theology or anything else. At the same time our variables admit of varying degrees, function positively and negatively, and allow for maximum cultural diversity. They are designed for comparative study, designed to help interpreters move from their own scripts to other scripts. The four cultural patterns provide four models of how different scripts work, allowing us to assemble otherwise disparate clues in theological statements into meaningful patterns.

IV. Strong-group/High-grid

Every application of this fourfold model should be seen as an experiment. To illustrate the model we begin with a relatively clear test-statement that might be made by some contemporary Catholic religious leaders: *the unbroken tradition of the church by which only males have been ordained to the priesthood is evidence of a divine intention binding on all generations of Christians.* The group-grid model makes us draw the following conclusions:

(1) The group will expressed in its practice is accorded ultimate validity. To construe church tradition as equivalent to divine intention indicates the presence of an extraordinarily strong group.

(2) "Priesthood" itself implies that members are ranked in a sacred order within the group. As is typical in strong groups, the status of individual members is determined by the group.

(3) Were we to probe further the notion of ordination at work we would find that the ordained are said to have a sacred and indelible character, conferred in the church's sacramental ritual. Tacitly, this implies something about the non-ordained. If the ordained are set above and apart, the non-ordained are ranked below, essentially dependent.

(4) Ordination, then, draws sacred lines of access to the divine; it organizes the group as an everlasting community, the kingdom of God. Persons are what the group says they are. *Outside the church, no salvation* means *apart from the group, nothing.*

This is an ideological statement—ideological in the neutral sense that all theology is ideology. How does it square with everyday experience? We might test this by asking for example: on what basis do they assert that the tradition is "unbroken"?

(1) Limiting priesthood to "males" anchors group practice in an empirical criterion: however arbitrary it may seem, the sex of one to be

ordained is a more objective qualification for ordination than education, piety, or any internal disposition. Ordination by God and the church appear to rest on natural foundations.

(2) Moreover, the fact of male dominance in most societies serves to confirm the church's sacred order. If the church has the capacity to set the style for society, as it did on this question, the confirmation is all the clearer. Theology and experience match. This is high-grid.

Strong-group/high-grid scripts presume there is a place for everyone and everything and that more often than not things are as they should be. The stronger the group and the higher the grid the less need there is to invoke authority. The less authority is invoked, the more tacitly it may be assumed, the more powerful it is. In strong-group/high-grid, whatever already exists is legitimate; those above provide for those below. Everyone has a permanent, indeed virtually immortal place. To accept without question both a fixed relationship to God and fixed means of access to God is to have a systematic and coherent understanding of everything significant, because everyone knows the channels from which all reliable wisdom and grace come. In such an arrangement, who God is appears almost as clearly as who is or might be ordained by the church. God "himself" presides within his kingdom, the church.

Once we advert to the fact that the tradition is spoken of as unbroken, we ask how the group would explain a contrary practice. It could happen only outside its world, outside the boundaries of the group called "church." Those acting contrary to the group will are not merely deviant members, they are "non-members," or to recall our quaint usage, "non-Catholics." To borrow a term from a similarly strong-group culture, the Soviet world, they are "non-persons."

V. Strong-group/Low-grid

If strong-group people come to be surrounded by "non-persons," their values will not be confirmed by the wider society in which they find themselves. Their grid is lowered. Low-grid groups, having relatively few opportunities to verify their beliefs in everyday life, tend to retreat to "other worlds," "worlds to come." They will explain the hostile world in which they find themselves, usually by judging it evil or under evil powers. They enact this judgment, constructing it socially, by devising rules to avoid the evil that surrounds them.

Jews dominated successively by Babylonians, Persians, Greeks, and Romans became increasingly focused on a reign of God that would put the nonbelievers in their place. Of course, the issue was always what sort of place that might be. Are the Gentiles (non-Jews) to worship in the temple in Jerusalem or merely to be overcome? Any answer given lacks empirical proof, which means that all answers are tentative. This is the low-grid predicament.

But because the question is unavoidable, each answer generates a passionate following until it is disproved or reinterpreted. Each reinterpretation leads to a new faction, overlapping and contending with other factions. Thus, we find not only Pharisees, Essenes, and Zealots, but factions within all these factions. Early Christianity clearly fits within this quadrant, a messianic faction that produced innumerable sub-factions. Factionalism is endemic to low-grid groups, about which we note the following:

(1) Whereas the high-grid group thinks in terms of its own practice alone, the low-grid group thinks in terms of opposition to the evil without that threatens its own life.

(2) Theology as a systematic statement of doctrine does not exist in the low-grid quadrant. Systematic statements presuppose a vision of a world in which the group values would be confirmed. While visions may be readily proposed, they are never confirmed. Low-grid groups, among whom we would find many that we might call revolutionaries and others that we might label reactionaries, envision a world in which the evil of the present world is negated. Implicitly, if not explicitly, their affirmations of belief set them apart from the world.

(3) Low-grid Christianity is volatile. The high-grid church looks back to writings passed down from the sub-apostolic period for a coherent message about who Jesus was and what the church was meant to be. It finds numerous calls to believe that "Jesus is Lord," and to repent before Jesus' parousia as Messiah. Titles and descriptions abound. The plot of Jesus' life may climax in his empty tomb (Mark) or in his being lifted up (John) or in his being seen as disciples break bread (Luke). The most orthodox modern biblical scholars are willing to speak of the "churches the apostles left behind."[5]

What were the core beliefs? Who governed these groups? Modern scholars often speak of early Christianity as sectarian and charismatic. Neither description is accurate (Malina 1984), although modern sectarians and charismatics are low-grid and modern low-grid charismatics frequently create strong-group sects.[6] A sect is a group that has broken with an established religious tradition, and charismatic leadership challenges the religious tradition. Modern charismatic leadership focuses on the unique and individual qualities or inspiration of its leader. Its foundation is individualist, weak-group. Each of the factions within Judaism, including the factions of early Christianity claimed to represent—not break with—the fundamental tradition better than any others. Each was a renewed Israel, not a new Israel.

Jesus, Paul, and others are presented as embodiments of obedience to the God of Israel, not as inspired revolutionaries. Their following comes from their reputation for faithful obedience, which is perhaps the core value of Judaism. The Gospels were written as defenses against the charge of nonbelievers that Jesus was cursed for disobedience. Jesus and Paul acquire a reputation rather than make claims for themselves. Of themselves they say, "I was sent—leaving the initiative to God or others. Others assign the titles and roles. A reputational leader is acclaimed by people who see him as the embodiment of its own values. These disciples do not see themselves as breaking with their past, and it is more accurate to describe such bands of disciples as factions dismissed or disregarded within their own religious traditions rather than as sects that have chosen to abandon their confreres.

Low-grid Christianity functions in a kinship or family pattern, not merely because all those Christians loved one another, but because—like non-Sadducaic Judaism—early Christianity could invoke no existing politico-social framework to verify its claims or enforce its convictions. Even God is Father until his kingdom comes. The elder or elders in any given "household of the faith" could not command. They might persuade, but the persuasion rested on convictions already held by the group, convictions the group did not expect to be confirmed in their everyday interactions with the dominant society. But they could live out these values within their own "household of the faith," in the world apart the group created.

VI. Weak-group Life

Almost thirty years ago Hannah Arendt observed "that authority has vanished from the modern world."[7] She asked "what was authority?" Her definition of *auctoritas* comes from Greco-Roman culture, and technically applies only within our strong-group/high-grid quadrant. The felt absence, a sense of deprivation, of such authority accounts for the defensive posture of the strong-group/low-grid quadrant. But a lack of both authority and even of any sense of loss about authority—even though we still use the word—is characteristic of weak-group culture.

To the extent that individuals establish their own identities, associations and values, they are weak group. In a court of law, the weak-group individual is innocent until proven guilty, while strong-group courts would try individuals presumed guilty until proven innocent. In other words, the individual is prior and group life rests on the voluntary adherence of individuals. Nonetheless, as we will see, the priority of the individual and the principle of voluntary association does not negate, and may even invigorate group life and theological development.

Douglas contends that the social body and the individual body tend to be seen in similar ways.[8] Where boundaries around groups are clearly defined, the individual body will be perceived as containing the person. Where group boundaries are undefined or considered unimportant, the person is more likely to be seen as inherently undefinable, unbounded. In other words, the soul, personality, or inner spirit will be seen as using its body and other bodies for its own transcendent purposes. Fixed relationships are minimal. One's sexuality, for example, provides only raw material that might be used in any number of associations. Weak-group people do not see human nature as realizable in a single human culture; they do not see cultural variations as unnatural deformities or evil. They see options.

Thus, weak-group Christians may be born into a religious tradition, but adherence to the tradition is a continuing choice, and nonadherence does not threaten them with nonpersonhood. The tradition provides personal meaning; it is not a fixed reality. This perspective is clear in most contemporary theological presentations. Quite pious theologians begin with our experience and situation asking how traditional beliefs and practices illuminate our lives, or they may begin with the beliefs and practices asking how they are relevant to our situation. We use the body of the religious tradition for self-fulfillment.

An often overlooked feature of weak-group people is that they are not merely individualists. Like strong-group people, they may be either high-grid or low-grid. Mainstream America is decidedly high-grid. This means our values are confirmed within the society in which we live. And the process of confirmation is intimately related to the process by which we form and maintain associations and groups. Indeed, the wider the range of group affiliations the higher the grid, because each group is a finite world in which some values are confirmed.

High-grid individuals frequently affirm some of the groups into which they are born, and easily affiliate with others. Their membership in a group is, in fact, a function of their willingness to participate in it, to assure its growth and development. In other words, they join with others, not because they naturally or necessarily belong with them, but to further common objectives already shared or to be developed. This task-orientation tends to assure that they will give themselves to those groups most likely to secure their goals and results in groups relatively likely to have the resources to achieve any goals decided upon. Needless to say, since goals are always open to redefinition, and groups always open to reorganization, the overall network of associations in which individuals participate provides a larger world in which many of their values are confirmed.

The larger world makes sense, because meaningful action takes place in relatively autonomous "worlds." The religious "world" relates to, but is not part of, the political or academic or economic "worlds." A plurality of finite "worlds" is negotiated by self-defining individuals. They may feel conflict, but conflicts are usually perceived as open to resolution by redefining priorities and objectives, rather than as matters of principle or fundamental values. This is possible because the ultimate values are internal to the individual, who functions as a free spirit within his various bodies.

The burden the weak-group cultural pattern places on the individual is considerable. . . . Transcendent meaning (which strong-groups embody and sustain on behalf of their members) must be found within the individual. To the extent that these individuals know that the groups to which they belong are their own creations, they may depend on them for validation to a finite degree. Their whole world may make sense, have meaning, but it does not have the appearance of necessary truth.

VII. Weak-group/Low-grid

Thus, weak-groups are also low-grid as well as high-grid. Indeed, phases of incoherence of low-grid serve a real purpose in the weak-group individual's achievement of a higher grid. Transitional stages, notably but not only adolescence, are periods in which weak-group people become aware of the mismatch between their own internal values and the bodies, physical and social, in which they must live. The extent to which they "drop out" of ordinary groups will vary, but it is through such experiences that the individual is prepared to be the free spirit intended.

The potential for more or less extended alienation becoming permanent is also present. The weak-group individual may be possessed of a unique genius or spirit at odds with all relationships readily available in the society. Such extreme isolation, in which ultimately the person within is satisfied with neither social or physical bodies, is difficult to sustain. If the mismatch between values and experience cannot be bridged, such individuals tend to gravitate towards one another, forming stronger bonds, a sense of loyalty at least to their inner uniqueness. They develop strong-group/low-grid characteristics.

In the weak-group/low-grid quadrant, for the same reasons as in the strong-group/low-grid quadrant, systematic theological statements are impossible. But this is the quadrant in which unique religious (and other creative) inspiration flourishes. Validation of this inspiration is at best momentary and on a one-to-one basis. What has been experienced at such great personal cost can be transmitted only in an equally personal way.

Douglas's four-quadrant model provides axes by which we can plot where different theologies lie culturally. The advantage of the model is that it arranges cultural data in terms of relationships between group and individual and between value statements and value experiences. This allows us to look at issues such as authority in terms of the dynamics created by these relationships rather than in terms of who holds it, how much it covers, and how well it might be received. Above all, it allows us to see that the need for something equivalent to *authority* is neither uniformly felt nor uniformly satisfied.

A final issue of great importance (that I must omit because of space limitations) is the fact that cultural scripts are wholes. The parts of any script are not interchangeable. *Yahweh* does not have a role in the *Summa Theologica* any more than American nuns do. When we abstract the details of cultural scripts into patterns such as Douglas conceived, we are able to see why this is so. The dynamics that hold elements of a script in place are not present in every script, and these patterns focus our attention on the basic dynamics, helping us to avoid the pitfall of letting translations of individual words seduce us into thinking anyone can think anything. At our best, we may grasp some of the reasons why other people think as they do. The more their experience diverges from our own, the less likely we shall ever be able to think their thoughts. Once that is recognized, we might be prepared to at least let them have their own thoughts, and theology, and even, if they have a place for it, authority.

Notes

1. Following quite different approaches, anthropologist Mary Douglas and philosopher Michael Polanyi reach similar conclusions on this point. Douglas says, "If we ask of any form of communication the simple question, what is being communicated? the answer is: information from the social system." See *Implicit Meanings* (London: Routledge & Kegan Paul, 1975), 87. Under the rubric of "conviviality," Polanyi describes the "sentiments of fellowship" that exist previous to articulation among all groups of men and even among animals in his book, *Personal Knowledge: Towards a Post-Critical Philosophy* (New York: Harper & Row/Torchbooks, 1958), 209.

2. The contention of Berger and Luckmann that the appropriate subject for the sociology of knowledge is "everything that passes for 'knowledge' in society," rather than ideas alone, is equally pertinent in religious studies. Ideas of God and religious authority, if not derived from common experience, are clearly woven into the fabric of that experience rather than self-existing creations of theological minds. See author, *The Social Construction of Reality: A Treatise in the Sociology of Knowledge* (Garden City, N.Y.: Doubleday and Co., 1966), 14-15.

3. A. B. Kernan, *The Imaginary Library: An Essay on Literature and Society* (Princeton: University Press, 1982).

4. B. Malina, *The New Testament World: Insights from Cultural Anthropology* (Atlanta: John Knox, 1981) and *Christian Origins and Cultural Anthropology: Practical Models for Biblical Interpretation* (Atlanta: John Knox, 1986).

5. R. E. Brown, *The Churches the Apostles Left Behind* (New York: Paulist, 1984).

6. B. Malina, "Jesus As Charismatic Leader?" *BTB* (14, 1984): 55-62.

7. H. Arendt, "What Was Authority?" in *Authority*, ed. C. J. Friedrich (Westport, Conn.: Greenwood Press, 1981), 81.

8. M. Douglas, *Natural Symbols: Explorations in Cosmology* (New York: Pantheon Books, 1982), 65-81.

Theology, Hierarchy, and Power

Ronald Pasquariello

Senior Fellow for Urban and Economic Policy
Center for Theology and Public Policy, Washington, D.C.

A MISSING DIMENSION IN THE DEBATE over the relationship between theology and authority in the Catholic Church has been an analysis of the influence of ideology. That ideology is present is frequently acknowledged: doctrinal disputes are usually seen in terms of liberals versus conservatives, for example. However, the ideology being addressed here is of a type different from that traditional dichotomy. This article intends to focus on hierarchy as ideology.

As will perhaps be always true in the Catholic Church, the issue is not just theology and power, or just theology and authority, but theology and hierarchy. There are obviously different kinds of power and different kinds of authority. In the Catholic Church, power's most frequent form is hierarchical.

Perhaps the proper question in the current debate is, How and to what extent can theology be true to itself as a science (in the widest sense) within a hierarchical structure? To bring some clarity to the debate, it is essential to understand hierarchy. "People order their universe through social bias. By bringing these biases out into the open, we will understand better which policy differences can be reconciled and which cannot."[1] It is the thesis of this essay that clarity can be brought to the theological discussion by bringing the ideological elements in the debate out into the open. Moreover, if theology is still in some way faith seeking understanding, then it is especially incumbent on the theologian to expose the presence of ideology in the faith, in regard to both doctrinal and theological statements.

This essay does not represent the ruminations of a discontented Catholic theologian who has chosen to zero in on some authoritarian elements in the Catholic Church and hold them up for ridicule by giving them the negative connotation that ideology has "enjoyed" since the time of Marx. Rather, it is based on the substantive and highly regarded work of cultural anthropologist Mary Douglas and political scientist Aaron Wildavsky.

We often think of cultures and ideologies in terms of great political or social or economic systems—Marxism, Maoism, nazism, liberalism, conservatism, capitalism, anarchism, classism, racism, sexism. Mary Douglas, (followed by Aaron Wildavsky) has made an important contribution to the understanding of culture and to ideology as a cultural system by defining cultures in these terms: hierarchical, egalitarian or sectarian, market individualist, fatalist.

Elements of this theory can be found in her work, which once enjoyed extensive popularity in the religious and theological community, *Natural Symbols*.[2] This analysis was further extended in her seminal essay, "Cultural Bias,"[3] and further developed by her and Aaron Wildavsky in *Risk and Culture*.[4]

While this essay employs the substantive research of these two scholars, the focus here will not be on hierarchy as a culture but as an ideology, i.e., as a construct of thought which legitimates the action taking place within a particular culture. An ideology, in this perspective, is a rationalization of a preferred cultural orientation.

From this perspective, hierarchy is a way of being, a way of orienting oneself to the world. It is one way in which certain people deal with the world, and other people when they deal with the world and other people—i.e., they deal with them hierarchically.

As an ideology and a cultural way of being, hierarchy applies to much more than the Catholic Church. It is being examined here, however, with the hope of bringing some light to the current doctrinal dispute within the Catholic Church. Recognizing its presence will help sort out the theological arguments from the ideological ones. It could also help move the debate from the ideological to the theological. This essay will not focus on all the elements of hierarchy, but on hierarchy as ideology, which is perhaps its most salient feature.

Catholics do not often think of hierarchy in ideological terms. We usually relate to it as merely a matter of church organization. Any organization, however, is more than just the arrangement of parts for the sake of order and smooth operation, or a bureaucratic arrangement for achieving certain objectives. An organization itself is a culture, a way of life replete with its own values, beliefs, rituals, and symbols interwoven about a bundle of desires and interests which are the *raison d'être* for the organization.

IBM, which not only sets up work rules, but legislates matters of dress and social decorum within and without the workplace, exemplifies a hierarchical corporate culture. IBM's corporate culture is highly individualistic and competitive. It differs, as we have become recently aware, from those well-publicized Japanese corporate cultures, which while hierarchical are structured around worker-manager cooperation rather than conflict. Aldous Huxley's *Brave New World* is another example of a hierarchical corporate culture; in that case, it is predominantly political. Corporate cultures are usually shaped by hierarchical ideologies. The Catholic Church—not a corporation, but a corporate culture—is also hierarchically organized.

I. What Is Ideology?

As Minogue warns, when it comes to ideology, "the academic enquirer walks straight into a minefield."[5] The exact meaning of ideology is elusive, perhaps because it has been overanalyzed; more probably, because it, like ants at a picnic, is everywhere, and gets into everything.

What is important, however, is the fact that it has been given so much attention because of its salience in shaping our lives together. Ideology is a powerful force, a potent instrument for good or evil, fraught, like a wild horse, with danger if it is not identified and bridled to the service of humans.

Perhaps most important for this essay, an ideology is a way of constituting power, of deciding who is in and who is out of group relationships. This is apparent in Minogue's identification of "the pure theory of ideology," which is "any doctrine which presents the hidden and saving truth about the evils of the world in the form of social analysis."[6]

Ideologies tend to divide the world into "us" and "them," the "good guys" and the "bad guys," the believers and the oppressors, those who are ideological partisans and those who are not. This is perhaps clearest to Westerners when one considers Marxism as an ideology. From that perspective, capitalism is the bad guy. It is no less true, however, from the capitalist perspective. Ronald Reagan gave it its clearest expression when he referred to the Soviet Union as the "Evil Empire," conjuring up associations with the Manichean world of Darth Vadar and Luke Skywalker of *Star Wars*.

From an ideological perspective, everyone—by virtue of class, sex, race, ethnicity, nation, etc.—is assigned to one side or the other. There is little middle ground. One is either an Aryan or not, a racist or not, a sexist or not. "America, love it or leave it" is an ideological expression of nationhood.

A clear look at the functioning of ideology is accessible from Minogue's broad definition of ideology. "More generally, ideology is the propensity to construct structural explanations of the human world, and is thus a kind of free creative play of the intellect probing the world."[7]

There are three important elements in this definition. It suggests, in the first place, that an ideology is chiefly an intellectual construct, though it may operate consciously or unconsciously, as most students of ideology admit.

Secondly, it is comprehensive, ultimately a doctrine about the systematic basis of the world's evils. Everything that happens is explicable in terms of the relevant ideological structure. It is a road map, as Geertz suggests in another context,[8] that transforms mere physical locations into places connected by numbered routes and separated by measured distances, and so enabling us to find our way from where we are to where we want to go. Ideologies are sources of information through which human life can be patterned.

Thirdly, ideology making is also a propensity of human nature. Everyone has an ideology (or ideologies, for several can be mixed), which is always in the process of construction and reconstruction. Every attempt to make sense out of the world is an ideological maneuver. Thus the factory worker, the member of the underclass, the academic, the corporate manager, and the political leader all have their own ideologies. The poor person who is fatalistic about her/his "station in life" is being ideological, as is the academic who claims that what the poor need is the "spur of their poverty" to change their economic status.

In addition, ideology has an inspirational message, calling upon people to take up the struggle for liberation, the oppressor being the one who does not accept or conform to the ideological structure. The prime example of the ability to take advantage—effectively, but dreadfully—of the inspirational aspects of ideology is, of course, Hitler. Ronald Reagan is another effective manipulator of the inspirational elements of the American conservative political ideology.

Simply put, through their ideologies people decide for or against authority. A rebuke or affirmation by authority, and a person's response to it, determines the line between what is rational or irrational, acceptable or unacceptable. We construct and reconstruct our ideologies through our decisions vis-à-vis authority. If we accept, we confirm the ideology. If we reject, then we alter it.

As Geertz points out, ideologies are culture patterns, i.e., "programs." "They provide a template or blueprint for the organization of social and psychological processes. . . ."[9] Culture in this sense is not to be understood in terms of its ethnic raiment, i.e., as national customs, but as methods of control, rules or proscriptions by which persons are to behave.

> Culture is best seen not as complexes of concrete behavior patterns—customs, usage, traditions, habit clusters—. . . but as a set of control mechanisms—plans, recipes, rules, instructions (what computer engineers call "programs")—for the governing of behavior.[10]

Thus in making a decision, a person is deciding for or against the authority of culture/or ideology, either in the form of a particular rule, or in response to the current decisions of group leaders.

The activity of a person is largely devoted to building and shaping ideology. The activity has a purpose—to justify desired social relations. The trips of Pope John Paul II may be looked on as an attempt of a leader to get closer to the people in order to understand better their situation, but they may also be looked on as an attempt to assert hierarchy, an effort to remind the people who their leader is.

In actuality, ideologies seldom exist in the pure form. In practice, they are obscured by contradictions, tensions, and inconsistencies. They are diffuse. From a few premises, people give shape to many consequences applicable to a wide area. Humans are "cognitive misers who have a limited capacity for dealing with information, and thus must use cues and previously stored knowledge to reach judgments and decisions as accurately and efficiently as possible."[11]

Ideology can have a positive aspect, even though it may be described negatively, as it often is.

> In its most developed form an ideology constitutes an explanation of the nature of man in the universe, a critique of existing society from the standpoint thus established, and a description and justification of the good or legitimate political and social order.[12]

Ideologies are the matrices in which behavior and understanding are shaped. They allow humans to filter selectively the chaotic barrage of sense impressions and ideas and actions that assault the psyche on a daily basis.

They are negative when they are imposed and when they distort the facts. An ideology is characteristically an incomplete picture of reality.

One sees only those aspects of a situation which suit one's intention and purpose. They are the product of selective perception, often directed at the status quo, which they perceive to be under attack. According to Mannheim,

> The concept "ideology" reflects the one discovery which emerged from political conflict, namely, that ruling groups can in their thinking become so intensively interest-bound to a situation that they are simply no longer able to see certain facts which would undermine their sense of domination.[13]

Thus ideologies often get wholly out of keeping with the realities of the situation.

II. Hierarchy As Ideology

The thesis of this essay is that intertwined among the components in the current debates within the Catholic Church that have to do with faith and doctrine—over which there is scant disagreement—are ideological elements, which are the major source of the conflict. Recent examples of these debates include: the controversy over the ordination of women to Roman Catholic priesthood, the disagreement over the meaning of the 1984 *New York Times'* statement on politics and abortion, the silencing of third world theologians, and the hierarchical repudiation of the writings of theologian Charles Curran on matters of sexual ethics.

An ideology is a complex of ideas, images, motives, dogmas, duties, values, memories, aspirations, symbols, and rituals. The way a person uses any one of these reveals his/her ideological orientation. Since ideology constrains—consciously or unconsciously—the way persons, particularly those who are the caretakers of authority, speak and act, it is helpful to distinguish three types of statements being made in the contemporary debate.

There are faith or doctrinal statements, such as, "Jesus Christ is risen from the dead." There are also theological statements: that indirect abortion—in the case where an attempt is made to save the life of the mother and fetus, and the fetus is aborted in the process—is permissible under certain circumstances, for example.

In addition there are ideological statements. These may vary with the ideology. Examples of hierarchical statements are the following: "Only men can be priests because Jesus was a man"; "The pope says . . ."; "It is the wish of this bishop that . . ."; "it is not his/her place to . . ."

None of these statements—faith, theological, or ideological—are mutually exclusive. Only the word of God that addresses us in these linguistic formulations is free of ideology, calling all ideology into question. Theological statements and faith statements can, as oppressed groups have taught us, have an ideological bias. For example, "Jesus is Lord" is a statement of faith. It intends to say something about the preeminence of Jesus among all humankind, but it also has overtones of patriarchical and racist dominance when it echoes in the ears of feminists and American blacks.

It should be noted that hierarchical statements need not be made by someone in authority to be ideological. Anyone, hierarch or "lowerarch," making these kinds of statements in a positive manner would be indicating her/his commitment to a hierarchical ideology. They are, in addition, characteristic of all contemporary religions, and of contemporary life in general, particularly of organizations.

The following are the main elements of the hierarchical ideology. They have been gleaned in various places from the writings of Douglas and Wildavsky cited above. Each represents a potential source of conflict: when hierarchy is imposed in disregard of the truth, it operates negatively. When hierarchy serves the truth, it acts positively and appropriately.

(1) Hierarchy is pro-leadership, the operative assumption always being that the leaders are the "upperarchs," i.e., those at the top. In any ideology, the basic questions are how, what, and by whom: *how* should the world be organized, *what* should be done and *by whom*. In a hierarchy, those at the top appropriate the powers implied in these questions for themselves. They are the ones who decide the answers to these questions. They take the initiative, and it is up to the lowerarchs to obey. As such, hierarchy is a form of institutionalized authority.

Since it is pro-leadership, leadership is the most important value, more important even than the whole, which is its *raison d'être*. Leadership is there to protect the interests of the whole, but it is also convinced that there is no whole without leadership. Leadership, therefore, is to be shored up at every opportunity—protected when under attack, shedding and diffusing blame, keeping information under close control.

(2) Another characteristic of hierarchy, is that the whole is more important than the parts or the sum of the parts. It is, in fact, greater than the sum of the parts. The parts are supposed to sacrifice for the whole, and it is the leaders who are the ones with the knowledge about what is best for the whole. Collective sacrifice, according to hierarchical understanding, will lead to group gain. Hierarchy constrains individu-

ality. Lowerarchs are to sacrifice for the collective.

Obedience is the primary requirement of lowerarchs. Initiative is replaced by team spirit. And it is those who play by the rules who make it to the top. When they get to the top, they expect the same response from lowerarchs that enabled them to get to the top. Achievement, i.e., getting to the top, confirms the hierarchical world view of those who "make it."

(3) Hierarchies reflect detailed divisions of labor. They are therefore highly regulated. Each person has his/her place in the scheme of things, and is supposed to act properly according to his/her role in the hierarchy. It is the job of the hierarchs to decide what is best for the whole, to rule; the lowerarchs are to obey. Hierarchs judge who has the right to do what is essential to hierarchy because it is necessary to maintain distances and differences within the organization.

(4) In a hierarchy, people lower down do have rights against those higher up. Certain areas exist in which the hierarchs may not transgress. The rights of higher ups in a military hierarchy, for example, are limited to exclude interference with family life.

(5) Participation is perfunctorily acceptable, with those higher up trying to channel it because high rates of participation undermine the role of those higher up, and complicate their jobs. Participation should be appropriate to one's role in the hierarchy. Competition or individual initiative is acceptable as a necessary evil, so long as people accept their ordained place.

(6) Hierarchy, because it cannot exist without a lowerarchy, institutionalizes inequality. It justifies inequality on the grounds that specialization and division of labor enable people to live together with greater harmony and effectiveness. Being fairly treated does not mean being treated like everyone else, but being treated according to the rules affecting one's own station in life.

(7) When it comes to blame, rather than blaming the system (for it cannot be wrong, admission of wrong putting the whole in jeopardy) hierarchy tends to blame individuals, who are considered deviants. When something goes wrong, instead of checking the system for faults, personal blame is heaped on those with inadequate socialization: They do not know their place. The deviant must reform and conform or be purged by censure or excommunication.

(8) Hierarchy emphasizes central planning. But even here, the planning is reserved to the hierarchs. Strengthening the center is better than fragmentation. Innovation is to emanate from the head. It figures

out the right thing to do as if the organization had a single mind. Others are brought in for consultation, though this is most often a perfunctory role.

(9) Interestingly, hierarchy takes an ambiguous position in regard to new information. Usually it resists new knowledge, because of its capacity to "rock the boat," i.e. introduce information that puts the authority of the hierarchs in a bad light. New knowledge also increases the desire for personal participation, presenting the possibility of other centers of power and the potential for lack of control by the hierarchs.

But hierarchy sometimes accepts new knowledge, realizing that it may be threatened when it is no longer in touch with new understandings. It reserves, however, the right to itself to decide what new knowledge is acceptable. So long as it does not mean rapid change—which might threaten hierarchical structures—hierarchy can and does make room for accommodations. It is slow to discard old information because appeals to memory or tradition preserve its legitimacy. Hierarchy returns to the old until the new can be accommodated within the existing order.

Knowledge is closely guarded, because it is a means of control. In a religious hierarchy, there is a tendency to see revelation as coming from God through the leadership.

(10) Hierarchies are very sensitive to short-run dangers to group cohesion. This is because they expect the system to cope with long-run or future contingencies just as well as in the past. To doubt this would be to doubt the system in which all hope resides. Bringing future decisions down to the present would add to the number of decisions that have to be made.

III. Conclusion

If ideological elements are present in the debate, it is important to identify them. Ideological statements are not matters of faith. When they are used to serve the self-interest of the ideologue, i.e., to distort facts to preserve a particular ideological position, then they must be identified as such and resisted.

However, one needs to know the ideology in order to be able to detect distortion. In order to sift out ideological statements, one must know the elements of the ideology. That is why this essay has focused on hierarchy as ideology, eschewing, for the time being, discussion of the other cultural orientations defined by Douglas and her colleagues.

Knowing the elements of the hierarchical ideology should serve as a road map through the current controversy. The major conflict is a conflict of ideologies—hierarchical versus egalitarian. Hierarchs demand loyalty, while egalitarians want a voice. Hierarchs emphasize authority; egalitarians, consensus. For hierarchs, authority is a function of status; for egalitarians, it is a function of ability. Hierarchs stress the importance of role and function, while egalitarians seek to reduce differences. Hierarchs blame the person; egalitarians, the system. For egalitarians, fair is equal; for hierarchs, fair is right order.

Ideologues do not necessarily know they are acting ideologically. Pointing it out to them may or may not meet with successful results, because when a person is acting ideologically, he or she is defending the system, not necessarily the truth. Facts such as the development of doctrine and its dynamics, for example, get sidelined.

To act hierarchically is to impose power for its own sake. Authority can be used reasonably within a hierarchical framework, if it tries to persuade instead of compel or coerce, and if it is constantly vigilant for the gentle winds of truth sweeping across human history.

Notes

1. M. Douglas and A. Wildavsky, *Risk and Culture: An Essay on the Selection of Technical and Environmental Dangers* (Berkeley: University of California Press, 1982), 9.

2. M. Douglas, *Natural Symbols: Explorations in Cosmology* (New York: Pantheon Books, 1982).

3. M. Douglas, *In the Active Voice* (London: Routledge & Kegan Paul, 1982).

4. Douglas and Wildavsky, 9. See also, A. Wildavsky, *The Nursing Father: Moses as a Political Leader* (Alabama: University of Alabama Press, 1984).

5. M. Minogue, *Alien Powers: The Pure Theory of Ideology* (New York: St. Martin's Press, 1985), 5.

6. Ibid., 2.

7. Ibid.

8. C. Geertz, *The Interpretation of Cultures* (New York: Basic Books, 1973), 216.

9. Ibid.

10. Ibid., 44.

11. P. J. Conover and S. Feldman, "How People Organize the Political World: A Schematic Model," *American Journal of Political Science* 28 (1984): 95-111.

12. W. T. Bluhm, *Ideologies and Attitudes: Modern Political Cultures* (Englewood Cliffs, N.J.: Prentice-Hall, 1974), 5.

13. K. Mannheim, *Ideology and Utopia* (New York: Harcourt, Brace Jovanovich, 1936), 40.

Episcopal Teaching Authority on Matters of War and Economics

8

James L. Heft, S.M.

Department of Religious Studies
University of Dayton

AMERICAN CATHOLIC CHURCH HISTORIANS emphasize that from the foundation of the Republic, Catholic bishops made a distinction between the spiritual authority of the pope, to which American Catholics were subject, and temporal matters, in which they were free to do whatever was necessary for good citizenship. In 1826, Bishop John England told Congress that American Catholics wished to be just like their fellow citizens except in matters of religion.[1] In 1960, John F. Kennedy assured a group of nervous Protestant clergymen that his own Catholicism would in no way influence the exercise of his duties as president. Religion and politics would be kept separate. Or, as it was put on the eve of the 1980 presidential election by the title of an editorial in *The New York Times,* "Private Religion, Public Morality."

But times have changed considerably, especially in the last few years. Both England and Kennedy would be forced to rethink their statements now that the American bishops have published a pastoral letter on the morality of nuclear war and are currently preparing one on the economy. The public reaction has been intense and varied.[2] Among Catholics, some are thrilled by what they perceive as a new style of leadership, one marked by humility and courage and free admission of its fallibility. Others are appalled that the leadership of their church is teaching through an episcopal conference when it has no authority to do so. Still others believe that although the conference may issue letters, it should only outline principles, leaving their application to those competent to apply them. Finally, some few are disappointed in the tentative character of the conference statements and would have preferred clear and binding statements, the sort that would have enhanced—they believe—the authority of the bishops.

The purpose of this paper is to reflect on three points: first, the teaching authority that bishops may legitimately exercise on matters of morality that have to do with war and economics; second, the kind of teaching authority that episcopal conferences may exercise in such matters; and third, the ecclesiological significance of the process the American bishops have engaged in to draw up these pastoral letters. In other words, using more technical language, I will consider what bishops can teach authoritatively, that is, the object of teaching authority; then the way in which bishops in national conferences can teach, that is, the subject of teaching authority; and finally, the role of the *sensus fidelium* in the formulation of authoritative teaching.

I. What Can Bishops Teach Authoritatively?

In their 1983 pastoral letter on war and peace, the U.S. bishops explained that they would "address many concrete questions concerning the arms race, contemporary warfare, weapons systems and negotiating strategies." But they immediately added:

> We do not intend that our treatment of each of these issues carry the same moral authority as our statement of universal moral principles and formal Church teaching. Indeed, we stress here at the beginning that not every statement in this letter has the same moral authority. At times, we assert universally binding moral principles (e.g., noncombatant immunity and proportionality). At still other times we reaffirm statements of recent popes and the teaching of Vatican II. Again, at other times we apply moral principles to specific cases (par. 9).

They then proceeded to explain that when they apply moral principles, they make "prudential judgments" based on specific circumstances which not only can change, but which people of good will can interpret differently. While admitting that their moral judgments in such specific cases (e.g., their treatment of "no first use") therefore do not bind in conscience, the bishops nevertheless ask that they be given "serious attention and consideration" (par. 10).

I shall limit myself to asking one question about these carefully nuanced statements of the bishops: at what level of authority are "universally binding moral principles" taught? In other words, could a person for good reasons dissent from such a "universally binding moral principle"? Put in another way, could a Catholic support the saturation bombing of civilian populations believing that such a tactic would in the long run save more lives? Put in still another way, can "universally binding moral principles" be taught infallibly, in which case no dissent may be possible without jeopardizing one's identity as a Catholic Christian?

The first conciliar discussion of the object of pastoral teaching authority took place at the Council of Trent (1545-1563) where the role of the bishops was said to include the preaching to their people of the faith that must be believed and put into practice. The bishops used the phrase "matters pertaining to faith and morals" *(res fidei et morum)*, which, according to Francis Sullivan, "indicates that while some matters of faith are simply to be believed, others are to be both believed and put into practice."[3] At Trent, the gospel was described as "the one, salutory font of truth and of moral teaching" *(fontem omnis et salutaris veritatis et morum disciplinae)*. Thus, the gospel is understood as the source of all saving truth and *disciplina morum* is understood best not as "moral discipline," as a literal translation would have it, but as instruction or teaching *(disciplina)* about *morum* or practices, which includes how we are to live and act and worship as Christians.[4] At Trent, *disciplina morum* included more than teaching about morals; it included as well matters of custom and ecclesiastical and liturgical discipline. Thus, the phrase *res fidei et morum* is best translated as "matters pertaining to (Christian) faith and practice."[5]

A more thorough discussion of the object of episcopal teaching authority took place at Vatican I (1869-1870). There it became clear in the discussion about the object of papal infallibility, that is, about matters of faith and morals, that there existed both a direct and an indirect object. In the official commentary *(expositio)*, Bishop Gasser, in the name of the deputation of the faith, explained it this way:

> As I said before, since other truths, which in themselves may not be revealed, are more or less intimately bound up with revealed dogmas, they are necessary to protect, to expound correctly and to define efficaciously in all its integrity the deposit of faith. Truths of this nature belong to dogmatic facts insofar as without these it is not possible to protect and expound the deposit of faith, truths, I repeat, that do not belong directly to the deposit of faith, but are necessary for its protection.[6]

According to Gasser then, infallibility extends first to those truths which are revealed, and then to those which are not directly revealed, but which are necessarily connected to revelation. The bishops at Vatican I had disagreed over the precise content of the indirect object of infallibility. They had agreed as to how those truths should be connected. Some of the bishops wanted the secondary object defined as "those things connected with the deposit of revelation," but others objected that this was too vague and could be interpreted to include almost anything. Gasser explained that it included only those truths necessarily connected to revelation. He noted the teaching of theologians that infallibility concerned only revealed truths, while other definitions were only "theologically certain."[7]

Vatican Council II (1962-1965) did not attempt to clarify further the secondary object of infallibility (see *Constitution on the Church,* Article 25), and since the Council the only official statement to touch upon the matter was *Mysterium Ecclesiae* of 24 June 1973, which restated the secondary object of infallibility in slightly different terms: "things without which the deposit cannot be properly safeguarded and explained" *(sine quibus hoc depositum rite nequit custodiri et exponi).*[8] Sullivan concludes his discussion of this matter in this way:

> While the fact that there is a secondary object of infallibility is held by most Catholic theologians to be certain, there is by no means unanimity with regard to what is contained in this object. I think it would be fair to say that many manuals of ecclesiology prior to Vatican II reflected the broad description of the secondary object as "truths connected with revelation." The current trend would be to limit this object to what is strictly required in order that the magisterium might be able to defend and explain the Gospel.[9]

Another way in which theologians have taken up this question is to ask whether the magisterium is able to teach infallibly about questions of natural law. After examining relevant portions of Gasser's official commentary on the texts of Vatican I, and after comparing a relevant portion of a preliminary draft proposed at Vatican II for the document on the church with the final approved text, and after analyzing portions of the minority report of the commission of experts appointed by Pope Paul VI to study the question of birth control, Sullivan concludes that particular norms of natural law are not the object of infallible teaching.[10] Catholic theologians have come to this conclusion not only because of the particular complexity of moral problems facing us today, but also because the gospel often provides light rather than specific solutions for which Christians, as well as others, must search long and hard.[11] Finally, if the particular norms of the natural law are not (in the framework provided by Vatican I) the object of infallible teaching, basic principles of the natural law are, even though it "does not seem that any such moral principle has ever been solemnly defined."[12]

If now, in the light of these considerations, we return to our original question, what conclusions can we draw? Can "universally binding moral principles" be taught infallibly? If Sullivan is correct, the answer would seem to be yes, but only if we are talking about basic principles of natural law, and specifically about those which have been revealed to us "for the sake of our salvation." The U.S. bishops illustrate what they mean by "universally binding moral principles" by citing as examples the principles of noncombatant immunity and proportionality, principles that require in their application the evaluation of complex specific circumstances, evaluations which in many instances could be legitimately disparate. This fact alone would seem to rule out the possibility that these principles could bind consciences, at least in their application, in the way in which basic principles of the natural law could bind. I will leave it to the moral theologians to enumerate and distinguish between basic principles of the natural law, which could be infallibly taught, and the particular norms of the natural law which can not. The very fact that moral theologians have not done this indicates the difficulties inherent in formulating moral principles that can be defined infallibly. Moreover, it would also be necessary to show that these principles, even before their application, have been revealed to us "for the sake of our salvation." No dogmatic theologian has to my knowledge ever attempted to demonstrate that.

II. With What Kind of Teaching Authority Can Episcopal Conferences Teach?

We have just established that particular norms of the natural law, the sorts of norms which would be most often employed in discussion about the morality of war and economic justice, cannot be a part of the secondary object of the infallible magisterium. We now turn to our second question: with what kind of authority can episcopal conferences treat matters of war and economics? It is commonly held in Catholic ecclesiology that the teaching authority of the hierarchy may be exercised in one of two ways: on the one hand, in an "extraordinary" way when a doctrine is defined by an ecumenical council, or by a pope speaking infallibly, or, on the other hand, in an "ordinary" way when a doctrine is taught by an individual bishop in his local church (see *Constitution on the Church,* Article 25). The authority of teaching is exercised legitimately therefore in either an extraordinary or an ordinary manner.

When the American bishops went to Rome in 1983 to discuss their pastoral on the morality of nuclear war, Cardinal Ratzinger said: "A bishops' conference as such does not have a mandate to teach. This belongs only to individual bishops or to the college of bishops with the Pope." Compared to the teaching prerogatives of individual bishops, Ratzinger said that "national conferences have no theological base."[13] Moreover, he stated that such conferences are merely practical expedients that run the danger of undercutting by bureaucracy and anonymity the personal teaching authority of individual bishops.

Several points need to be made in view of the remarks of Cardinal Ratzinger. First, Vatican II acknowledged and encouraged the establishment of limited expressions of collegiality. At the end of Article 23 of *The Constitution on the Church*, for example, it is stated that modern episcopal conferences can contribute fruitful assistance in the development of a deeper collegial sense.[14] Articles 37 and 38 of the *Decree on the Bishops' Pastoral Office* underscore the importance of episcopal conferences by likening them to the synods, provincial councils and plenary councils that achieved so much good in the early church. Concerning the teaching authority of episcopal conferences, Article 753 of the new Code of Canon law states:

> Although they do not enjoy infallible teaching authority, the bishops in communion with the head and members of the college, whether as individuals or gathered in conferences of bishops or in particular councils, are authentic teachers and instructors of the faith for the faithful entrusted to their care.

Article 753 appears in the section of the Code that deals with the church's teaching function. Therefore, recent official statements of the Catholic Church do offer a theological basis for episcopal conferences exercising a legitimate role as authentic teachers.

There is also strong historical precedent for episcopal conferences that teach with authority. Particular councils have contributed in significant ways to the development of doctrine. One needs only to recall, among many possible examples from the early church, that the provincial council of Carthage issued in 418 the first decrees on the subject of original sin, and that the council of Orange in 529 condemned semi-Pelagianism, and from more recent history, that the episcopal conferences of Latin America have issued important statements at Medellin in 1968 and at Puebla in 1979. In view of this, it would be difficult, in the opinion of Avery Dulles, "to defend the view that there is no teaching authority between the universal magisterium of the popes and ecumenical councils, at the one extreme, and that of the individual bishop in his own diocese at the other."[15] After explaining that episcopal conferences do not, according to Vatican II, exercise a magisterium in the strict sense, Archbishop James Hickey of Washington, D.C., spoke about the impact of the teaching of episcopal conferences while address- ing a meeting of the American bishops at Collegeville in June of 1982:

> . . . one would have to be quite blind and deaf to reality if he denied that the statements of episcopal conferences do have an effective impact on the pastoral life of local dioceses and beyond. How many have not relied on the pastoral letters of episcopal conferences to find pastoral solutions to burning moral issues? How many times are priests and people not referred to the teaching of our conference and of other conferences? Many of the pastoral letters of conferences play an important role in the life of the Church. We have to admit, then, that the conference offers a most effective vehicle nationally for our teaching office.[16]

It is of course important that national episcopal conferences avoid nationalism which would weaken the unity of the universal church.[17] Moreover, they are not to substitute for the voice of the individual bishop, but rather to strengthen it by providing a coherent framework within which complex issues may be addressed more effectively.[18]

It should be plain, then, that episcopal conferences do have a solid historical and theological basis. It is also clear that they exercise a legitimate and authentic teaching authority. One question, however, remains: in the strict sense, do they have a "mandate to teach"? Some theologians, including Cardinal Ratzinger, have answered negatively and have based their response on what they maintain is a strict reading of the documents of Vatican II and the new Code of Canon Law. They state that episcopal conferences are not given the capacity to engage in "truly collegial acts," acts that are given only to the pope united with the bishops in a council, or to all the bishops dispersed throughout the world but acting in union with one another and the pope.[19]

In response to such an argument, it needs to be remembered that one of the rules for the strict reading of any official document of the church is, "never assume that an answer has been given by a text to a question which was not raised when that text was formulated." At Vatican II there was no discussion of whether episcopal conferences had a "mandate to teach." The Council encouraged the establishment of episcopal conferences. Now that they have been established and are having a definite impact on the life of the church, the question of whether they have a "mandate to teach" naturally arises. The question is an open one. If one bishop teaching in union with other bishops and the pope has a "mandate to teach," it seems reasonable that even more so an episcopal conference which teaches in union with other bishops and the pope should have a "mandate to teach." An episcopal conference does not, of course, have "the authority proper to the whole episcopal college together with the pope."[20] Nevertheless, as Article 753 of the new Code states, the bishops, individually or gathered in conferences, are "authentic teachers and instructors of the faith for the faithful entrusted to their care." Indeed, we may come to conclude that episcopal conferences exercise a mandate to teach situated somewhere midway between that exercised by the individual bishop and that exercised by the bishops and pope gathered in council.

III. The Expanded Role Given to the *Sensus Fidelium*

The establishment in the last twenty years of both episcopal conferences and the international synod of bishops has created promising forms of collaboration among the hierarchy. One of the most significant dimensions of the way in which the U.S. episcopal conference has chosen to work is the process it used to draft the pastoral letter on nuclear war and is using again to draft its letter on economics. The committees responsible for drafting these letters have consulted a wide variety of people. Preliminary drafts were made public so that criticisms could be made and suggestions offered with a view to preparing a second draft, which again would be criticized and discussed before submission for a final vote—article by article—to the members of the episcopal conference. Several comments should be made about this process. I shall limit myself to three: first, the way it indicates a new role for the laity; second, the way it calls for more persuasive teaching; and third, the way it points out the importance of noninfallible teaching.

Without ever defining what infallibility actually is, the bishops of Vatican I did say that it was the same infallibility that belongs to the church as a whole. We know that the consultation of the laity through their bishops played an important role in the definition of the two Marian dogmas.[21] The bishops of Vatican II made it even clearer that the infallibility of the pope and bishops had to be related to the "sense of the faith" possessed by the entire people of God:

> The body of the faithful as a whole, anointed as they are by the Holy One (cf. 1 John 2:20,27), cannot err in matters of belief. Thanks to a supernatural sense of the faith which characterizes the People as a whole, it manifests

this unerring quality when, "from the bishops down to the last member of the laity," it shows universal agreement in matters of faith and morals. For by this sense of faith which is aroused and sustained by the Spirit of truth, God's People accept not the word of men but the very Word of God (cf. 1 Thess. 2:13). It clings without fail to the faith once delivered to the saints (cf. Jude 3), penetrates it more deeply by accurate insights, and applies it more thoroughly to life.[22]

It is important to note the four effects of the *sensus fidei* mentioned in the article: (1) the people accept the word of God for what it really is; (2) they adhere to the true faith without ever falling away from it; (3) they are enabled to penetrate more deeply and elucidate more clearly that revelation; and (4) they are able to apply the word of God more thoroughly to life. When we consider the issues of the morality of war and economic justice, it should be evident that the competencies of the laity must play a central role in the shaping of these teachings, especially if these teachings are going to include applications. It also seems evident that the bishops responsible for overseeing ("episcopacy") the drafting of such documents will need to depend upon the competencies of the laity to grasp more clearly and with greater insight the ways in which the gospel is to be applied to these modern complex matters.[23]

Closely related to the "sense of the faith" is the "sense of the faithful." If the *sensus fidei* is more of a subjective quality of believers, the *sensus fidelium* carries a more objective meaning which refers not to the believers but to what they believe. The importance of the "sense of the faithful" was pointed out by Newman when he showed how it was precisely the laity who had faithfully clung to the truth in the face of the Arian crisis. It is the recognition of the importance of that same "sense of the faithful," that moved another English cardinal, George Basil Hume, to speak on 29 September 1980 at the International Synod of Bishops on the Family about the necessity of consulting the laity on such matters. He explained that the prophetic mission of husbands and wives is based on their experience as married people "and on an understanding of the sacrament of marriage of which they can speak with their own authority." Both their experience and their understanding constitute, the cardinal suggested, "an authentic *fons theologiae* from which we, the pastors, and indeed the whole Church, can draw."[24]

Many theologians who write today about consulting the laity write also about the way in which teachings acquire authority through their reception.[25] There is a tendency in our democratic society to reduce the matter of consulting the laity to the taking of a majority vote or settling for the least common denominator. At the other extreme is the perception common among non-Catholics, and unfortunately among not a few Catholics as well, that papal and episcopal statements acquire their authority only because popes and bishops make them, and not also because the statements are true. Neither democracy nor autocracy exemplifies the process by which teaching acquires authority in the Catholic tradition. There is rather a subtle but important interplay, yet to be sufficiently worked out by theologians, between, on the one hand, formal (who says it) and material authority (what is said), and on the other hand, the way in which the acceptance of a teaching affects its authority. Suffice it here to say that important insights into this complex matter will be found in a deeper grasp of the nature and function of the "sense of the faithful."

A second new emphasis in the church is the need for more persuasive teaching. In the last twenty-five years a shift away from an emphasis upon formal authority (who says it) to one on material authority has occurred. This becomes all the more necessary when we are dealing with moral matters that depend to a considerable extent upon the interpretation of the natural law, such as is the case with matters of war and economics. As Sullivan explains, "When the (moral) norm itself is said to be discoverable by human reasoning, it would be a mistake to rely too heavily on merely formal authority in proposing it for acceptance by thinking people."[26] The more people are consulted, the more the final result embodies the wisdom of the community, the more likely it is to be accepted by that community.

A third aspect of the new situation in the church in North America is the discovery of the value of fallible teaching authority. In the past, most Catholics expected their bishops and the pope to speak infallibly or to remain silent. The new dialogical mode of proceeding employed by the American bishops in drafting their most recent pastoral letters openly calls for help and expects to learn a good deal through the process. The bishops in using this method have stated that some of their conclusions may be wrong and expect and respect divergent opinions on matters of application. This mode of operating is perplexing for those who prefer their bishops to speak in absolute ways or to remain silent. We all need to recognize that in many of the most important areas of our life we must rely upon discernment rather than infallibility to indicate for us the right way to live. In 1967, the German bishops put the matter well:

> . . . human life, even at a wholly general level, must always be lived "by

doing one's best according to one's lights" and by recognised principles which, while at the theoretical level they cannot be recognised as absolutely certain, nevertheless command our respect in the "here and now" as valid norms of thinking and acting because in the existing circumstances they are the best that can be found. This is something that everyone recognises from the concrete experience of his own life. Every doctor in his diagnoses, every statesman in the political judgments he arrives at on particular situations and the decisions he bases on these, is aware of this fact. The Church too in her doctrine and practice cannot always and in every case allow herself to be caught in the dilemma of either arriving at a doctrinal decision which is ultimately binding or simply being silent and leaving everything to the free opinion of the individual. In order to maintain the true and ultimate substance of the faith she must, even at the risk of error in points of detail, give expression to doctrinal directives which have a certain degree of binding force, and yet, since they are not *de fide* definitions, involve a certain element of the provisional even to the point of being capable of including error. Otherwise it would be quite impossible for her to preach or interpret her faith as a decisive force in real life or to apply it to each new situation in human life as it arises. In such a case the position of the individual Christian in regard to the Church is analogous to that of a man who knows that he is bound to accept the decision of a specialist even while recognising that it is not infallible.[27]

The bishops cannot afford to remain silent about matters on which they cannot speak infallibly. How specific they should become in what they say may well be debated.[28] Whether they should speak at all should be obvious from what has been written here.

IV. Conclusion

First, we have concluded that bishops can teach infallibly only in regard to basic principles and not the particular norms of the natural law. We noted that it is commonly agreed that no such basic principles of the natural law have ever been infallibly defined. Second, we concluded that episcopal conferences have in fact had powerful impacts through their teaching activity and have in the process recreated in the church a variety of expressions of collegial cooperation and activity. Moreover, whether they ought to have a mandate to teach remains an open question. Finally, we have described three new developments in the interaction between the hierarchy and the laity: a more important role for the laity, an emphasis on more persuasive teaching and a deeper appreciation of the value of noninfallible teaching authority. These developments are, of course, causing a good deal of confusion within the church, something not unexpected when there is a change in the way of doing things. With the new initiatives of the bishops and the greater involvement of the laity addressing issues that in fact constitute the structures of everyday life for all citizens, the "sense of the faithful" will be called upon more than ever to penetrate the gospel and apply it more thoroughly to life as it is actually experienced and lived.

Notes

1. D. J. O'Brien, "American Catholics and American Society," in *Catholics and Nuclear War,* ed. P. J. Murnion (New York: Crossroad, 1983), 18.

2. See D. Hollenbach, "Notes on Moral Theology: The Bishops and the U.S. Economy," *TS* 46 (1985): 102.

3. F. A. Sullivan *Magisterium: Teaching Authority in the Catholic Church* (New York: Paulist, 1983), 128.

4. M. Bevenot, "Faith and Morals in the Councils of Trent and Vatican I," *HJ* 3 (1962): 15-30.

5. Sullivan, 128. He insists on the word "Christian" to emphasize the fact that for Trent not only the "salutary truth," but also moral teaching *(disciplina morum)* has the gospel as its source.

6. G. D. Mansi, *Collectio Conciliorum,* vol. 52. (Paris: Petit and Martin, 1899-1927), col. 1226.

7. Mansi, 52:1316-17. See G. Thils, *Infallibilité pontificale: Source, conditions, limites* (Gembloux: J. Duculot, 1969), 246, and Sullivan, 133.

8. Pope Paul VI, *Mysterium Ecclesiae* in *Acta Apostolicae Sedis* 65 (1973), 401.

9. Sullivan, 134.

10. Ibid., 140-47. For a spirited argument against Sullivan's conclusions and for the possibility of infallibly defining particular norms of the natural law, see G. Grisez, "Infallibility and Specific Moral Norms," *The Thomist* 49 (1985): 248-87. Grisez argues that adultery and abortion could be infallibly condemned. His disagreement with Sullivan concerns the teaching on contraception. My concern in this essay is moral principles that have to do with war and economics.

11. Sullivan, 151.

12. Ibid., 149.

13. See *The Tablet* 238 (8 December 1984): 1223.

14. Article 23 of *Lumen Gentium* speaks of episcopal conferences as helpful ways to develop a "collegiate spirit" *(collegialis affectus),* a phrase that has led, in the words of Charles Murphy, to a distinction between "effective and affective" collegiality: " 'affective' referring to the exercise of supreme power in strictly collegiate acts; 'affective, describing more of an atmosphere of mutual co-operation, assistance and love among the bishops"; see "Collegiality: An Essay Toward Better Understanding," *TS,* 46 (1985): 40.

15. A. Dulles, "Bishops' Conference Documents: What Doctrinal Authority?" *Origins* 14 (32, 1985): 530. Since Ratzinger's statements in December 1984 concerning episcopal conferences, Dulles and a few other theologians have cited Ratzinger's article published twenty years ago in the first volume of *Concilium* (New York: Paulist, 1965) on "The Pastoral Implications of Episcopal Collegial-

ity" in which the then young German theologian and *peritus* of Vatican II argued for a more effective exercise of collegiality through episcopal conferences.

16. Sullivan, 121-22.

17. H. De Lubac has written about this danger in *Particular Churches and the Universal Church* (San Francisco: Ignatius Press, 1982). Concerning the differences of approach among the pastorals of the American, French and German bishops on war and peace, see J. Heft, "Do the European and American Bishops Agree?" *The Catechist* 18 (October, 1984): 20-23.

18. Bishop J. Malone, "The Intersection of Public Opinion and Public Policy," *Origins* 14 (24, 1984): 388.

19. See Murphy, 38-49.

20. Sullivan, 122.

21. J. Heft, "Papal Infallibility and the Marian Dogmas," *Marian Studies* 33 (1982): 59-63, reprinted in *One in Christ* 18 (1982): 309-40.

22. *The Documents of Vatican II*, ed. W. M. Abbott, S.J. (New York: Herder & Herder, 1966), 29-30.

23. *The Documents of Vatican II*, 64-65.

24. G. B. Hume, "Development of Marriage Teaching," *Origins* 10 (18, 1980): 276.

25. On the idea of reception, see A. Grillmeier, "Konzil und Reception, Methodische Bemerkungen zu einem Thema der oekumenischen Diskussion," *Theologie und Philosophie* 45 (1970): 321-52; Y. Congar, "La réception comme réalité ecclésiologique," *Revue des sciences philosophiques et théologiques* 56 (1972): 369-402; E. Kilmartin, "Reception in History: An Ecclesiological Phenomenon and its Significance," *JES* 21 (1984): 34-54; M. O'Gara, "Infallibility in the Ecumenical Crucible," *One in Christ* 20 (1984): 325-45 and T. P. Rausch, S.J., "Reception Past And Present," *TS* 47 (1986): 497-508.

26. Sullivan, 165.

27. Ibid., 156-57.

28. I agree with B. Benestad, *The Pursuit of A Just Social Order: Policy Statements of the U.S. Catholic Bishops 1966-1980* (Washington, D.C.: Ethics and Public Policy Center, 1982), who distinguishes between social teaching and policy statements, and recommends that the bishops limit themselves to the former unless it is clear that only one policy is consistent with the gospel.

Stages of Authority:
Küng vs. the Vatican in Fowler's Categories

9

Michael Barnes

Department of Religious Studies
University of Dayton

T HERE ARE TWO DIFFERENT AND OFTEN OPPOSED ways of dealing with
the topic of authority in the Catholic Church. One of these is
from the perspective of theology, in which the doctrines concerning
the authority of tradition and the authority of the magisterium take a
preeminent place. The other perspective derives from the social sciences, in which the place of authority is more open to question and
in the case of psychology is as often attacked as supported.

Psychological analyses of religion have complained of the authoritarian bent in religion at least since the time of Hegel.[1] From Feuerbach
to Freud to Erich Fromm the psychological analysts have decried the
tendency of religious believers to seek a superior power which will guide
their lives, thereby relieving them of the burdens of personal responsibility.[2] Now James Fowler's analysis of the stages of faith development
appears to confirm more empirically what others previously claimed,
namely, that reliance on authority is not merely different from a more
autonomous stance but represents a deficiency in human development.[3]

The work of investigating the stages of faith development has only
just begun. What follows here then includes a fair amount of speculation
based on Fowler's writings and also on those of Piaget, Kohlberg, and
James Rest.[4] It will take much more research to test the validity of
these and other interpretations.

I. The Stages of Faith

Of the six stages which Fowler describes we can skip over the first and
sixth, on the grounds that only a very young child represents the first

stage and that the sixth is largely hypothetical, invented by Fowler to cover very rare religious individuals. The middle four stages represent patterns that are found in the lives of ordinary adults. A quick sketch of them will highlight the differences and allow for a comparison with types of theology.

Fowler's stage 2, which he calls the *mythic-literal* stage, is first roughly achieved by the average school-child, growing in complexity presumably as the child experiences more and more of the world.[5] As in all the stages it is not the particular content of belief and morals and behavioral forms that reveals the stage of faith or understanding or morality. It is rather the way in which a person possesses these. For the stage-2 person reality is constituted increasingly by a story line, a narrative, that is perceived to be the one, single, conglomerated truth. The person is trapped, as it were, in the narrative, because the person cannot recognize it as a narrative, one story among alternative stories, but can only see it as how things are.

In this world there are authoritative sources and authority figures, the reality of whose authority forms part of the narrative. Thus a nine-year-old learns that the Bible is God's word and that parents and priest have the correct understanding of it, and that is the simple truth. I will call this the literal stage. It is a literalism that is pre-fundamentalist in that it does not yet perceive a need to defend the one right interpretation against others. It more naively just absorbs all sorts of ideas into a conglomerated assembly of truths about reality.

In stage-3 consciousness, called *synthetic-conventional* by Fowler, there is the beginning and then the development of awareness of alternative narrative or stories.[6] The origin of this consciousness apparently lies in the initiation of what Piaget called formal operational thought, a style of thinking that begins to entertain more hypotheses about alternative possibilities and which can begin to mentally test hypotheses to see how logically coherent they are.

This intellectual development presents a problem for life. How can a person achieve coherent unity and direction in the midst of many conflicting possibilities? The major reference and support for the stage-3 person in this project is not yet the explicit criterion of logical coherence. That will come with stage 4. Instead it is the authority carried by the social-familial group to which the person belongs, an authority often attached to specific leaders with authority roles in the group. Let me call this simply the loyalty stage.

This would more typically represent many a Protestant fundamentalist.[7] It also represents, I believe, the average Catholic traditionalist who is highly sensitive to the issues of group identity and authority figures in that group. According to this attitude, when the pope says something, Catholics must simply obey; and a tendency in the church to be fought vigorously is the Protestantizing one, which blurs the distinction between Catholic identity and other group forms.

There are inevitably some conflicts between the traditional norms of group identity and the statements of authority figures. Thus an Archbishop Lefevbre rebels against a Pope Paul VI whom he sees as not sufficiently Catholic according to traditional authoritative doctrines. A given authority figure, however, might accumulate enough prestige to have more leeway. Pius XII could legitimize the rhythm method of birth control by just an allocation to Italian midwives.

Such conflicts within the group could be one of the factors propelling a person out of stage-3 and into a stage-4 style of consciousness, in search of a way to adjudicate among conflicting interpretations. Stage-4 style, called *individuative-reflective* by Fowler, might also be labeled logical thought in intellectualist terms.[8] There is a greater ability to formulate a sense of self and the world in terms of an explicit and logically coherent worldview. The narratives and traditions a person has received must now meet a new test, that of logical coherence. They are often demythologized, i.e., translated from pictorial story form into a more abstract and logical form such as can be found in a religious philosophy or theology. Where once it was mainly other people, the group as a whole as well as authority figures authorized by the group, now it is also rational coherence that stands as a norm of what is true or false, right or wrong.

Fowler claims that in this stage a person often has excessive confidence in the power of the mind to possess the truth through its own rational analyses. The norms and beliefs of traditional or group authorities need not be lost to this person, but they must now fit with the requirements of rational analysis. The control over beliefs and morals exercised by scholastic theologizing represents a significant historical instance of this, I believe.

The fifth stage is called *conjunctive* by Fowler.[9] It is one in which the limitations of logical thought become more apparent. In this stage dialectical awareness comes to the fore wherein the ambiguity inherent in life and the inability of any conceptual system to finally overcome that ambiguity is accepted. Fowler uses the word "wisdom" to label the norm of authority, a wisdom, I would presume, which represents the results of a cumulative tradition, which in turn expresses a still ongoing process of human experience and reflection.

It would seem that each of these stages of development would produce a distinctive kind of theologizing. Any given theologian might provide a theology that mixed many sources and included many considerations and which, therefore, would not purely represent just one style of stage-consciousness. Yet a person's stage of consciousness could still be the determinative factor of the sort of theology that is done.

Theology can be done with a stage-3 approach. In this case a person would accept as a given the truth of tradition and authority and the doctrines they present. The project of theology would then be to elaborate more the inner meaning of what is already known or to discover any and all available arguments that might prove convincing to a critic or outsider that the doctrines are intrinsically true. In actuality the truth of the doctrines for the believer would be already settled. As we will see, the Conference of German Bishops, in a letter to Küng (17 February 1975) seems to presuppose this kind of approach. The model of theology provided is that first the church speaks, and then theologians are to find reasons to justify what the church says. [10] For some theologians systematic theology operates in such a fashion.

Another theology might represent a stage-4 kind of consciousness. In this case the theological argumentation would not merely explicate any reasonableness that could be discovered in a doctrine already accepted from authority, but would, to some extent, test the doctrine by the best rational standards available. In the history of Christian doctrine the way in which the doctrine of God was first made to fit the philosophical understandings available through the Neoplatonic model and then later in scholasticism through Aristotelian categories serves as a good example of this.

Still another theology might represent a stage-5 consciousness. An example would be current foundational theologies or correlational theologies. One distinctive aspect of such theologies concerns their willingness to genuinely question the grounds of any beliefs or belief system in the light of the historical character of all human knowing. How thoroughly and in what ways this questioning presses against belief varies. The different positions taken on the nature of theology by the various theologians in Swidler's book, *Consensus in Theology?* illustrates this. Each finds different ways of affirming the importance of the tradition, of Christian sources, of Christian experience, and of classical Christian texts. Also, each finds different but similar ways of granting

full critical power to common human experience as well as scientific—
i.e., historical-critical methods. Avery Dulles says here, for example,
that exegetes' and theologians' critical and creative role includes calling
attention "to what they see as deficiencies in past doctrinal formulations
and strive to mature the judgment of the church on questions currently
under discussion."[11]

All of this fits also with Fowler's claim that stage-5 consciousness
includes a second naivete.[12] This consciousness recognizes the symbolic
character of all discourse, even that of the more abstract language of
philosophy and theology. Myth and symbol now appear again, in the
form Tillich would call "broken myth," recognized as mythical or symbolic but also as necessary to give some expression to the mysteries
with which religion is concerned.

This sketch of the stages of faith development and the kind of
theologies related to each includes some speculation on my part. Only
further empirical investigations could determine its validity. Nonetheless even these speculations can provide a framework for sorting out
and illuminating some aspects of the authority conflicts that take place
in the Catholic Church. A specific case study can illustrate this.

II. Küng and the Congregation for the Doctrine of the Faith

The story of Küng's conflict with the Vatican is fairly well documented.
In English one finds the documentation entitled *The Küng Dialogue*,
translated and published in 1980 for the United States Catholic Conference Committee on Doctrine. This compilation was originally made
by the Conference of German Bishops with the cooperation of the
Vatican Congregation for the Doctrine of the Faith. It includes all of
the official correspondence from all sides. In addition Leonard Swidler,
with the cooperation of Hans Küng, edited a larger book entitled *Küng
in Conflict* (Image, 1981), which contains unofficial but related materials
such as the "Declaration of 1360 Catholic Theologians on the Freedom
of Theology" (pp. 27-30), as well as most of the material already in
The Küng Dialogue. There is a striking and consistent difference in the
way doctrinal and authority matters were handled on the two sides of
the dispute.

Some differences in style between Küng and the Vatican congregation
are to be expected regardless of any stage development. The adversaries
here, if I may call them that, have different responsibilities. As a
university theologian, Küng is supposed to question and speculate and

argue. As the body responsible for church doctrine, the Vatican congregation has to worry chiefly about maintaining doctrine with maximum clarity and continuity. But in addition to this difference in responsibility, I believe there is also a difference that is comparable to differences in stages of faith development. The Vatican congregation, I believe, could have carried out its responsibility in a different way. It could even have withdrawn Küng's *missio canonica* and declared him wrong in his theology, but with a different sort of approach than the one that appears generally in its statements. This kind of justification that the congregation habitually used makes a Fowler-style analysis relevant.

The differences in style between Küng and the congregation may be related to stages of faith development, but not in a way to suggest that Küng and the congregation follow genuinely different stage styles in their own modes of expression. One observes a degree of cumulativeness in regard to the developmental process.[13] The attitudes and styles of earlier stages need not be lost but can be subsumed into a different perspective as a person develops. A person who has a fairly well developed stage-5 mode of consciousness can nonetheless still appreciate the relative validity of abstract theology to sort out inconsistencies and to analyze and synthesize coherent positions. The same person can also have group loyalty feelings, such as a love of the church, and some sense of the value of authority figures in various social settings, such as an appreciation of the positive role the papacy can play in exerting leadership as in matters of social justice.

In practice this could mean that a public position, such as the one taken by Küng or the congregation, might deliberately appeal to a stage-3 group sentiment and sense of group authority, or to the need for theological consistency that is of more concern to a stage-4 consciousness, but still also include arguments or attitudes of the sort that are more indicative of a stage-5 dialectical approach. Public documents often make appeals on various levels to various parts of their audience all at once, regardless of the primary orientation of the people who produce the documents.

All this could make it impossible to classify documents according to the stage-consciousness they represent. But in spite of this, in the instance of the conflict between Küng and the Vatican congregation, stage-consciousness differences do appear. It looks as though Küng and some others in the dialogue argue as a stage-4 or stage-5 consciousness might, but that the congregation usually restricts itself to styles most consistent with stage-3, the loyalist style.

First of all, the congregation more readily seems to assume that doctrines of the church are bedrock references, as it were, solid and stable and unmovable, in need of no further argumentation or reformulation. What past councils have declared, as in the issue of infallibility, seems to be both clear-cut and nonnegotiable; one need merely compare a new theological opinion such as those which Küng offers to the established doctrine, to see whether the opinion is true or false. One needs some intellectual analysis, the congregation says, in order to clarify just what the new opinions are, but further theologizing will not affect the doctrines in any way.

One sees this in the approach of the congregation to Küng concerning his ideas on church and Eucharist (6 May 1971) and on infallibility (12 July 1971 and 4 July 1973).[14] The congregation keeps repeating that the doctrines are clear and true and asks Küng to show how, in the light of those doctrines, he can hold the opinions he does. The standard is made fully explicit in a 30 March 1974 letter to Küng which declares that the purpose of the investigation about his ideas is to clarify Küng's position so that an accurate comparison can be made with true doctrine, one which Küng must accept, not argue about.[15]

By contrast, Küng's approach consists in argumentation, not just about his opinions but about doctrines. His reply (21 June 1971) to the letter on church and Eucharist briefly argues the point at stake and invites further argumentation.[16] In his replies to the letters on infallibility he approaches the issue of infallibility not simply as a settled doctrine but with the kind of questions appropriate to a more critical theology.[17] He says that he seeks to know the grounds of the doctrine of infallibility so that a defense of the doctrines can be made.

The significance of historical conditions in interpreting doctrine functions as a disputed question between the congregation and Küng. The statements made by the congregation as a rule do not acknowledge the historical character of faith assertions. The sole exception to the rule occurs in the document *Mysterium Ecclesiae* of 24 June 1973. Part V of the document affirms that historical conditions affect every expression of revelation.[18] This was no small thing for the congregation to say, Cardinal Volk of Germany, a member of the congregation, later told Küng.[19]

The congregation carefully and strongly counterbalances this, however, with an insistence that though the expressions of revelation may change, the meaning of the doctrines does not change.[20] The congregation explicitly rejects the notion that dogmatic formulas offer changeable approximations to the truth. That would be "dogmatic relativism," it asserts.

The congregation also later complains when Küng suggests that both of them let the issue rest and let history determine the truth between them. "It is difficult to see how such a defined doctrine could be left to the judgment of history."[21] The congregation says that they cannot accede to a proposal to "veil or conceal the unambiguousness and clarity of the doctrine of faith." They apparently have no difficulty in knowing the clear meaning of doctrine.

By 15 February 1975, almost a year later, the congregation finally declared flatly that some of Küng's ideas about infallibility, the magisterium, and the Eucharist contradict church doctrines, and that Küng should cease teaching them. In response Küng argued that the congregation has not made its case. The "Declarations have not disproved anything which I had to say on theological grounds."[22] Küng, however, does acquiese for a time after this in not raising the points at issue publicly.

The impasse continued, then, with the congregation sure that it knew the church doctrines clearly and unambiguously enough and could refute Küng's position merely by contrasting his position with their understanding of the doctrines. Küng, on the other hand, appealed to different methods of settling the issues. He had insisted on a theological analysis of the grounds which could support the doctrine and which would also determine its meaning.

Interpreting all of this is risky, but as far as I can tell the congregation statements are stage-3 style in their reference to authoritative doctrines already sure and clear enough that no theological problems can override them or call their currently accepted meaning into question. Küng's approach is one a stage-4 consciousness would produce. The lack of good rational grounding, he claimed, made the congregation's understanding of the doctrines unsupportable and therefore not correct. The authority of official statements suffices for the congregation. The demand of rational analysis has an additional and determinative authority for Küng. Whether or not Küng's orientation also represents stage-5 considerations does not emerge clearly from the documents used here, though his concern for historicity suggests this.

III. The Value and Legitimacy of Stage-Analysis

The use here of stage-analysis might be invalid or irrelevant, as was

stated earlier, because it fails to consider how the purpose of the documents in question might dictate their approach. The congregation does
not have the task of doing theology, but to defend doctrine. The further
purpose to this, as the congregation noted, concerns the faithful. They
need clear guidance, not the open-ended uncertainty of theological
disputations.[23] The style of the statements by the congregation may still
represent a conscious choice to speak simply and authoritatively rather
than with more theological subtlety or historical consciousness. But
there are alternative ways of being clear without speaking so untheolog-
ically and unhistorically. And since the letters to Küng are the least
likely to be read by the faithful, it is there that the congregation could
be less absolutist in expression. It turned out that it was only in the
publicly disseminated *Mysterium Ecclesiae* that they acknowledged the
historical character of doctrine at all.

Let me offer a suggestion as to how they could have spoken more
theologically and historically to Küng and still have functioned as firm
defenders of received doctrine. They could have done what they did
do in their 1975 statement, and that is to tell Küng they were sure he
was in error on the issues named. But they might have expressed themselves something like this:

> After consultation with you and other theologians we are convinced that
> your interpretation of the doctrines at issue is not consonant with what has
> been the teaching of the church. In order to carry out our responsibility to
> safeguard the doctrines we have received, we find it necessary to state this
> publicly so that it will be clear that your opinions on these matters are
> theological speculations not yet in accord with current church teaching. We
> trust that in your writing and teachings you will make clear the difference
> between your own ideas and the understanding of this congregation, and we
> trust that you will find it possible to support us in bearing our difficult but
> important responsibility of recalling to the minds of the faithful as clearly
> as we can the doctrines of the faith.

It is not important here whether this wording is very good. And as
there exists no particular reason to believe that Küng would have been
satisfied with a statement such as this, the congregation might well
have ended up removing his canonical mission anyway. But this sample
statement does illustrate the fact that the congregation could publicly
defend doctrines in such a way as to accept the legitimacy of theological
speculation as such, and leave open the possibility of reinterpretations
of doctrine in the future. Neither critical theological argumentation
nor the reality of historical development find any apparent legitimacy

or significance in the congregation's statements generally as they currently stand.

IV. Some Reflections

All this brings us to the most difficult issue, the one raised at the beginning: the conflict between a theological approach and a social science approach. If this stage-analysis has any psychological validity, it may nonetheless lack any theological validity. To claim that psychologically speaking the congregation speaks with a stage-3 consciousness may miss the point that the congregation speaks, in a sense, as God has directed.

That is a strong way of putting what remains nonetheless part of much theology concerning the magisterium. Councils of the church have declared certain doctrines to be divinely revealed truths. In that case no theological analysis or historical considerations, much less psychological analyses, can ever tell against them. Such analyses may help to explicate more of their meaning, but their authority and meaning come from God, not from the use of human reasoning or from the relative historical conditions of the times in which they were formulated. Moreover, the authority of the magisterium in reaffirming the doctrines bespeaks a divinely established authority and not the authority of human logic or wisdom. This, at least, seems to be Catholic doctrine.[24]

The nature and authority of the magisterium need to be discussed here. I am not competent to do that. What I can do is use the stage-analyses to pose some provocative questions to those who are competent in the theology of ecclesiastical teaching authority.

The stage-analysis suggests that much of the traditional theology about church authority (including topics Küng and the congregation disputed concerning infallibility and the magisterium) has been a stage-3 type of theologizing. Kohlberg and Rest discovered that people at a given stage of moral reasoning could not understand more advanced stages. If this holds true of stages of faith development, then many who do a stage-3 type of theology may not be able to see it as a form of theology but simply as adherence to the truth; they would not be *able* to recognize the validity of alternative and more developed forms of theology.

If this is correct, then a stage-analysis such as I have used here is not necessarily just something different from a theological approach. It could also be a legitimate guide as to which theological approach is more satisfactory or valid. Where stage-3 theologizing would exclude the legitimacy of social science criticism of divinely grounded truth, stage-5 theologizing would accept social science analysis as part of the process of correlational theology, incorporating what is known from experience, historicity, limitations, and cognitional processes as an element in interpreting the specifically Christian sources of self-understanding.

To give one quick and awkward example of this: Vatican II asks the faithful to give "religious submission of mind and will" to "the authentic teaching authority of the Roman Pontiff, even when he is not speaking *ex cathedra.*" This too strikes me as a stage-3 understanding of authoritative teaching, one which overrides the responsibility for intellectual honesty and the evident fact of the historicity of all formulations (not to mention the fallibility, *per definitionem,* of all statements that are not *ex cathedra*). To have to accept such a statement literally would put a person in the position of having to choose to be either intellectually immature or dishonest. The best that I can do is to treat it as a stage-3 theological formulation, precisely one of the cases Dulles's words could apply to when he said that past formulations sometimes need correction. The connection in this and similar cases, I would hope, should be in the direction of stage-5 understanding.

The last problem is how to express and communicate a stage-5 understanding in a way that is meaningful to stage-3 and 4 consciousness. As I indicated earlier it would seem possible to appeal to stage-3 loyalty, to stage-4 logic, and also stage-5 historicity all at once. Ideas need to be expressed in such a way so as to acknowledge the legitimacy of logic and historical consciousness even though both of them offer a critique of the tradition as it has been understood up to now.

Notes

1. G. W. F. Hegel, *Early Theological Writings* (Philadelphia: University of Pennsylvania Press, 1948), 182-204.

2. E. Fromm, *Psychoanalysis and Religion* (New Haven: Yale University Press, 1950), 36-55.

3. J. Fowler, *Stages of Faith* (New York: Harper & Row, 1981). Fowler would probably choose a softer word than deficiency.

4. J. Piaget, *The Psychology of the Child* (New York: Basic Books, 1969); C. Kohlberg, *The Psychology of Moral Development* (New York: Harper & Row, 1984); J. R. Rest, *Development in Judging Moral Issues* (Minnesota: University Press, 1979).

5. Fowler, 135-50.

6. Ibid., 151-73.

7. Robert W. Shinn shares this interpretation in *Fundamentalism Today,* ed. M. J. Selvidge, (Elgin, Illinois: Brethren Press, 1984), 91-98.

8. Ibid., 174-83.

9. Ibid., 184-98.

10. *The Küng Dialogue* (Washington, D.C.: U.S. Catholic Conference, 1980), 96.

11. In *Consensus in Theology* (*JES*, 1980), 44, A. Dulles first argues against departing from the "approved doctrinal norms to the ecclesial body to which one belongs, but interprets this by denying that one begins with recent magisterial statements as an absolute norm, and then promotes the critical role of theology.

12. Ibid., 198.

13. See J. Rest, 48-74 for evidence that this is true in regard to moral development.

14. See *The Küng Dialogue*, 44-46, 48-51, and 60-61.

15. Ibid., 78-84.

16. Ibid., 46-48.

17. On 24 January 1972 and 22 September 1973 respectively. See *The Küng Dialogue*, 52-60 and 69-77.

18. Ibid., 193.

19. The declaration of the German bishops in this matter speaks of the historical nature of doctrine. Cardinal Volk of Germany could have convinced the congregation to include this idea (*The Küng Dialogue*, 96).

20. Ibid., 194.

21. In a letter to Küng on 30 March 1974. See *The Küng Dialogue*, 83.

22. *The Küng Dialogue*, 100.

23. In a letter to Küng on 30 March 1974. See *The Küng Dialogue*, 82-83.

24. In this regard see F. A. Sullivan, *Magisterium* (Mahwah, New Jersey: Paulist, 1983).

Theology and Authority: The Theological Issues

10

Richard Penaskovic

Department of Religion
Auburn University

I N THE AFTERMATH of the Second Vatican Council there was a new spirit of vibrancy and vitality in the church. The church seemed to enjoy a rejuvenation or second spring partly as a result of the reform or *aggiornamento* inaugurated by the Council.

Twenty years after the Council, one observes another swing of the pendulum. The exclusion of women from the priesthood, the inquiries into the works of distinguished theologians such as Schillebeeckx, Küng, and Curran, and the calling on the carpet of liberal bishops such as Hunthausen are all signs of a return to authoritarianism in the church. Many observers now speak openly about the fact that the ecclesiastical powers-that-be operate in bureaucratic fashion.[1]

The recall of Hans Küng's *missio canonica* in 1979 is particularly instructive in this regard. Essential elements of due process and justice, such as the right of the Küng to read the *acts* and to choose his own defense counsel were lacking. Equal rights were not granted to each party, as Wolfgang Seibel observes.[2] As a result of the Küng case the church came off in public opinion as a totalitarian institution that squelches individual freedom and allows no deviations from the official line. Instead of bringing about church unity which the authorities in Rome wanted, the case of Hans Küng had precisely the opposite effect; it increased the polarization in the church.[3] Some observers feel that the Curran case will further polarize the U.S. church in similar fashion.

Most theologians speak about the relationship between theology and authority solely in terms of the relationship between the teaching authority of the church (the hierarchical magisterium) and the theological magisterium.[4] I believe that the context into which the debate should be conducted needs to be widened. Theologians need to take into account the teaching authority of the community of faith. In a Latin American context, attention should be paid to the lives and thoughts of the poor, which are often the practical and theoretical equivalent of what the fundamental Christian dogmas are saying.

In a North American and European context we need to listen to the witness and thoughts of an educated and sophisticated laity mindful of the fact that all the great reform movements in church history were begun by the saints at the grassroots level. Ignatius of Loyola, for example, was thought to be heretical when he reformed the church. He was thrown into jail three times at the hands of the Inquisition and had to undergo trials in Paris, Venice, and Rome.[5]

When speaking about the relationship between theology and authority, both theological and canonical issues are intertwined. I make no attempt to deal with the canonical questions, neither do I treat all of the theological issues. Part one of this essay deals with these two theological questions, the church as the people of God and the development of doctrine issue, whereas, part two offers some suggestions for a renewed teaching office in the church.

I. The Church as the People of God

Competing Models of Ecclesiology

Today the relationship between the teaching authority of the church (the magisterium) and the theological magisterium (those theologians who investigate questions of faith in a scholarly way) is a strained one. The present controversy between authority and theology seemingly reflects two competing ecclesiologies namely, *democratic* and *institutional*. To elaborate, the way in which the church understands itself determines the manner in which it perceives the relationship between the hierarchical magisterium and the theological magisterium.[6]

What has prompted these two models of the church to be at loggerheads with one another? Some members of the hierarchy and the Roman Curia still seem to be operating under the *institutional model* of the church. This model stresses continuity between present and past, emphasizes certain virtues such as obedience, downplays critical thinking, and encourages clericalism whereby the laity are thought to have a passive role in the church.[7]

For the institutional model, authority resides either in the teaching office (magisterium) or in the theological authority of scientifically trained men and women (theologians). Ever since the Enlightenment in the eighteenth century, however, authority has been identified in a one-sided way with authority established on the basis of intellectual knowledge. Partly as a result of this development, the word "magisterium" has been used to refer only to the official authority in the church.[8]

The second model of the church, the *democratic model,* was elaborated by Vatican II in the Dogmatic Constitution on the Church. In this model priority is put on the church understood as the people of God. The Dogmatic Constitution on the Church discussed people of God *before* it spoke about the official authority in the church, thus reinstating the New Testament and the ecclesiology of the early church to a position of honor.[9]

In this model the teaching office in the church is understood in the context of the teaching authority of all believers. The Dogmatic Constitution on the Church sees the magisterium as subordinate to the word of God as found in scripture and tradition. The magisterium was placed in a fuller context in which other bearers of the Christian faith such as the liturgy, spirituality, and the sense of the faithful all have their own roles to play.[10]

Today we see the rise of nonacademic theologies. These ways of doing theology do not find their immediate context in academic theology but in the Christian community of faith. One observes this development in the case of the various liberation theologies that have commenced in the past twenty years.[11]

These base communities are increasingly becoming the active subject of the expression of faith. The magisterium of the church has not known what to make of this development and therefore has been wary of liberation theology as exemplified in the one-year silencing of Leonardo Boff. Instead of a simple clash between the magisterium and the theologians we now have on our hands a third entity, the teaching authority of all believers which has a certain preeminence vis-à-vis the magisterium and the theologians. The implications for the church as an institution have not yet been drawn from this. Consequently, the teaching authority of the community of all believers sometimes suffers from the powers-that-be in the church.[12]

The teaching authority of believing Christians regarding the doctrinal expression of faith occurs on a different level than the authority of the magisterium. The teaching authority of believers is also more difficult to define than the authority of the magisterium. It finds its location in the *sensus fidei*, (the sense of the faith). The *sensus fidei* of the whole church is much richer, more differentiated, and more active than the statements of the magisterium by themselves. Why so? The life of the church is sustained not only by the statements of the magisterium but by the gifts or charisms of the Holy Spirit, who inspires not only church leaders but also the laity.[13]

Public Opinion and Reception

When speaking about the teaching authority of all believers two notions—in a theological discussion at least—must be examined. The first has to do with "public opinion" in the church, the second with "reception."

Public Opinion. The importance of public opinion in the church was noted by John Henry Newman in his *Lectures on the Present Position of Catholics in England*, written in 1851. Newman said that the laity have the obligation of cultivating public opinion. For Newman public opinion has ecumenical relevance in that he sees the laity in a position to change the attitude of Protestants to Catholics.[14]

Public opinion in the church exists to make known what the people in the church are really feeling so that church authorities can take this into consideration in terms of their own actions. In other words, public opinion in the church is one important means whereby church authorities find out what the Christian people actually think and feel, what they find problematic in the teachings of the church, where they find the traditional answers deficient, and the like. It seems that the greater the number of people involved in the church, the more diverse they are culturally, and in terms of mentality, the greater the need for public opinion to exist within the church.[15]

If public opinion is to operate effectively in the church then Catholic laity and theologians must make their views known. If the people of God cannot freely speak then church authorities run the risk of leading the church behind soundproof ivory towers, says Karl Rahner. Of course it is a judgment call on the part of church authorities in terms of setting the limits to the free expression of public opinion in the church. However, as Rahner observes, the history of the church abundantly demonstrates that these limits have been set too narrowly in the past.[16]

There are circumstances in which the people of God have a real duty to speak out in the church, even though in so doing they may incur the wrath of the powers-that-be. It may even be the will of God that those who do speak out like Daniel and Marjorie McGuire may live for a time under a cloud because they represent a spirit out of the ordinary. Ultimately such a spirit may derive from the Holy Spirit.[17]

Reception. In speaking about the teaching authority of believers in the church, mention should be made of a new theological category, "reception." The popular theological dictionaries do not speak of reception. It derives from the history of law and has been used as a theological term only since 1968. Reception is a correlative concept, correlative to the councils of the church. The more encompassing a church council is received, the more ecumenical that council is. Reception, then, is a process of recognition and of confession vis-à-vis a council of the church.[18]

Reception is a never-ending process of reflection about the faith carried on in faith by the entire community of believers. Church authorities, academic theologians, and the people of simple faith are all included in this process of reception. The decrees of an ecumenical council may be true; however, instead of contributing toward a vibrant faith, they may prove to be a hindrance to it. The Fifth Lateran Council, for example, concluded in 1517 with almost the same reform program as Trent. Nonetheless, the former had no appreciable influence on the life of the church. Professor Franz Wolfinger says the same thing applies, making the necessary changes, to Vatican I. Instead of bringing about a living faith, the definition of papal infallibility in 1870 created more problems than it solved.[19]

Perhaps we need to look at the notion of reception analogously. It may be useful to consider it not only in connection with church councils but also in regard to the reception of encyclicals and declarations of the magisterium. An example may illustrate matters.

In *Humanae Vitae* Pope Paul VI said that Roman Catholics may not use contraceptives. His encyclical was poorly received. Resistance occurred on two levels: (1) theologically it lacked support, because many bishops and theologians felt that it was based on inadequate premises; and (2) practically the decision has little effect because many Catholics did not, and do not, feel themselves bound by it.[20]

What should be said about this nonreception of an official encyclical? Does it indicate moral weakness or does it express in a considered way the spontaneous reactions of the people of God? Is this nonreception a sign of the emergence of a different teaching from the traditional teaching of Pope Paul VI? Again we are faced with the question as to the authority of public opinion in the church.[21] I mention this point only to move on to another.

The Development of Doctrine

Another reason for the strained relationship between the magisterium of the church and certain liberal theologians has to do with the development of doctrine issue. What we have are two different, competing theologies.[22] Today's controversy is simply the continuation of the clash between two opposing theologies at Vatican II.[23]

What Vatican II did was renounce the monopoly of scholasticism in Catholic teaching, thus returning to the more concrete and historical model of the church fathers, as Yves Congar observes. This conflict between the neo-scholastic, ahistorical theology of the Roman School and the more historically conscious theology of more liberal theologians has surfaced in all areas of doctrinal and biblical theology; and especially today, it is visible in issues of moral theology.[24]

In regard to the authority question, neo-scholastic Roman theology views authority as the basis of stability and order. In this context "order" means that the lower is subordinate to the higher, everything in its proper place. This understanding of authority stresses stability and order, leaving little to change, uncertainty, or open-endedness. The model used to depict revelation is that of a deposit. So theologians spoke of a "deposit of revelation" or a "deposit of faith" which was complete from the beginning of the church. Thus the task of both the magisterium and the theologians is to preserve what has been received.[25]

Such a theological scheme allows for virtually no sense of any development from New Testament times to the present. Dogmas become concretized as timeless and unchanging formulations of the Christian faith. One could argue that the inability of Roman speculative theology to come to terms with the problems posed by the modern historical method and exegesis prevented the Roman theologians and the Roman congregations from understanding the questions which the Modernists tried to answer.[26]

One observes a similar situation in the church today. The names have changed but many of the issues remain the same. Instead of Loisy, Tyrell, and Schell being reprehended by Rome, we have Hans Küng, Eduard Schillebeeckx, and Charles Curran. Again, we have two competing theologies at loggerheads. Any disagreement with the theology espoused by the Congregation for the Doctrine of the Faith automatically becomes interpreted as an attack upon the authority of the church. A very limited theology, that of the Roman congregations, now becomes the touchstone by which other theologies are judged.[27]

Another source of disagreement between the hierarchical magisterium (consisting largely of bishops who teach by virtue of the authority
of office) and theologians (those who investigate questions of faith in
a scholarly fashion) concerns questions the magisterium has only seemingly settled. However, these dogmatic questions are presented as if
they were definitely settled forever. The failure to recognize these open
questions, argues Rahner, leads to a narrow interpretation of those
dogmas that do require assent, an interpretation that discourages further
discussion.[28]

In speaking about open questions which the institutional church
considers already answered, I am referring to the authentic statements
of the church's magisterium which traditional scholastic theology at
least up to Vatican II called *theologice certa* (theologically certain) on
the basis of common agreement among theologians. An example may
clarify matters. One may not say with certainty that the threefold
division of church office (the episcopate, the presbyterate, and the
diaconate) is of divine law since this division was not made by the
historical Jesus. Hence, it is not certain that Protestant churches would
have to adopt this division of pastoral ministry if they wished to be
united with the Roman Church.[29]

Perhaps we need to return to some of Schleiermacher's ideas in regard
to the development of doctrine. Schleiermacher had an extraordinary
sensitivity for the tradition of the church. Yet his model of doctrinal
development also emphasizes the creative abilities of the theologian as
a significant factor in the process of doctrinal formulation.[30]

The individual theologian, says Schleiermacher, is responsible both
to the orthodox past of the church and the church's present faith.
Schleiermacher's model of development puts a premium on the creativity and imagination of individual theological talent while, at the same
time, suggesting the responsibility of the church to the theologian.[31]

There is an irony to the vocation of theologians. The very tradition
which fosters the talents of theologians, the church, is often a tough
taskmaster and critic. Church authorities look suspiciously on deviations
from the orthodox tradition of the church. Hence the theologian is
like the artist whose innovations are misunderstood by contemporaries
and only appreciated in the history of art from the vantage-point of
temporal distance.[32]

There is one final point to be made about the development of doctrine
issue. The problem arises in an era of rapid technological change. In
a technological world truth functions as a future category in that more

will be known tomorrow, hence more can be done tomorrow. Truth does not consist in what can be received from the past but in what lies ahead. Such an approach to reality involves a lack of interest in, and even a break with, the past. Some students tend to have such an attitude and thus find it hard to respond to a historical treatment of a subject in theology.

However praiseworthy it may be to be open to the future, such an attitude when transposed to the study of theology has deleterious consequences. To break cleanly with the past in theological studies is catastrophic. Such an attitude when linked with a radical criticism of everything that smacks of the institutional does not bode well for the church.[33]

Technology understood as the application of organized knowledge for achieving specific and practical purposes also affects our communication. Communication satellites relay events happening at the far end of the globe into our living rooms. In the past both infallible and noninfallible statements of the pope were criticized only after a relatively long delay. The dialogue with the rest of the church in regard to papal encyclicals, for example, now occurs in a matter of days.

Formerly criticism took decades to unfold. Centuries elapsed before the teaching of the pope's direct power over all temporal matters was rejected. For many centuries the popes justified the immorality of torture. In fact, torture was practiced in their names and was condemned by Pius XII only after a long period of time. Today no major theologian can speak or write on an important issue without its being known the same day by almost anyone in the world who cares to know. Rapid and instantaneous communication makes this possible.[34]

II. Toward a Renewed Magisterium

To advance the discussion in regard to the question of authority, I offer the following observations from the perspective of systematic theology. I do have a genuine respect for the teaching office of the church. These remarks should be understood in the sense in which they are written — out of genuine love for the church.

(1) The magisterium of the church needs to remember that it has primarily the positive charge of encouraging the development of sound doctrine. In so doing it needs to perform its mission in such a way that the principle of subsidiarity is respected. In this connection subsidiarity simply means a bias in favor of the maximization of participation in

decision making in every sector of the church.[35]

The principle of subsidiarity holds two important implications for the teaching office in the church, more specifically, for the Congregation for the Doctrine of the Faith. One, Rome should promote regionalism instead of being wary of it. It could accomplish this by establishing national or regional conferences of bishops who could make binding regulations.[36]

Speaking to the United States bishops at Rome in regard to their pastoral on the morality of war, Cardinal Ratzinger, head of the Congregation for the Doctrine of the Faith, said that bishops' conferences have no mandate to teach (*mandatum docendi*). For Ratzinger national conference of bishops have no theological base and are in danger of undercutting the personal teaching authority of individual bishops.

Ratzinger's remarks are hard to square with Article 23 of the Dogmatic Constitution on the Church, which says that episcopal conferences can effectively contribute to the development of a deeper collegial sense. His remarks also run counter to Article 753 of the new Code of Canon Law, which states that episcopal conferences exercise a legitimate role as authentic teachers and instructors of faith for the believing community.

I would argue that if one bishop teaching in union with other bishops and the pope has a mandate to teach, even more so does an episcopal conference which teaches in union with other bishops and the pope. The point is well made by James Heft who concludes that episcopal conferences exercise a mandate to teach situated somewhere midway between the pope and bishops in council and that exercised by the ordinary individual.[37]

The second implication of the principle of subsidiarity is this: allow theological disputes to be settled on the regional level wherever possible, either by the national conferences of bishops or by the theological community. It seems to me to be almost a principle that error is exposed by the collision of mind with mind.

In the thirteenth century, for example, when the church was at the height of its temporal power, it was by freedom of discussion among theologians and not by intolerant opposition that the movement known as neo-Aristotelianism was eventually checked. Similarly, the tendency to identify extreme conservatism with orthodoxy caused a vigorous opposition to the "novel" intellectual movement known as scholasticism.

What we need today is a return to the theological community in order to resolve theological disputes. Both at Trent and in the eighteenth century the competency of theologians was institutionally celebrated. In the nineteenth century, (at least from the end of the Napoleonic War until Vatican I in 1870), the papacy asserted control over the previously semi-independent national churches. Part of the move toward *de facto* papal primacy involved papal intervention in theological matters. As the role of the pope increased, the role of theologians decreased in corresponding fashion. In this connection two points must be borne in mind: (a) the nineteenth century saw the introduction into theology of the term, magisterium; and (b) to the magisterium were ascribed divinelike characteristics such as the guarantee of the Holy Spirit to the pope. The upshot of this development in the nineteenth century was this: papal and episcopal competency were separated from the rest of the church.[38]

(2) If the magisterium is to be taken seriously in today's world it must find a new operational mode, that of offering guidelines rather than recalling the canonical mission of individual theologians. Because of the explosion of knowledge we have many complicated questions, particularly in regard to morality, such as genetic engineering, nuclear energy, and overpopulation. Such thorny questions do not admit of easy answers. Perhaps all the magisterium can do is offer some general guidelines or propose interim solutions.[39]

Vatican II called us a pilgrim church. This is especially the case in regard to questions of morality. Perhaps we are facing the situation of the *Ecclesia dubitans* or doubting church, that is to say that cogent and compelling reasons can be given for compulsory celibacy and its opposite, for the ordination of women and against it.

For this reason the teaching office of the church must be more circumspect today than it has been in the past. The magisterium should come out in the open and say outright that not all of its authentic statements carry the same weight.[40] One may, for instance, distinguish three levels of authority in the Pastoral on War and Peace issued by the bishops of the United States: (1) the authority of general moral principles, (2) church teachings, and (3) concrete applications.

Rome might want to take its cue from the process involved in drafting the recent statements of the United States' episcopal conference. These documents were discussed publicly then modified as a result of input from all sectors of the community of faith. This process indicates that not everything is evident in regard to such issues as war and peace or economics.[41]

In dealing with complicated questions of morality, the magisterium ought to listen to the views of theologians. The theologian represents the world and its constant movement of knowledge before the church. As the intellectual in the church, the theologian confronts church doctrine and ethics with all the new insights produced by the changing, historical nature of the human mind.[42]

What should theologians do if they disagree with noninfallible church teaching, such as the church's view on abortion? Is it enough to maintain an obedient silence? What concretely does respect for the magisterium entail? May theologians register their dissent publicly?[43]

I believe that theologians have the right to and even the obligation to dissent publicly from noninfallible church teaching. If, for example, all theologians had kept quiet in regard to the biblical decrees of Pope Pius X, then the present pope would never have been able to speak of the "J" source in Genesis.[44]

(3) Why does not the Congregation for the Doctrine of the Faith (CDF) call on the International Theological Commission to help it in dealing with such cases as that of Leonardo Boff? Moreover, the theologians who work for the CDF should have an international reputation and should be representative of the pluralism found in theology today.[45]

If the magisterium took seriously the above suggestions, its own authority would greatly increase rather than decrease.

Notes

1. C. Duquoc, "An Active Role for the People of God in Defining the Church's Faith," in *The Teaching Authority of the Believers*, ed. J. B. Metz and E. Schillebeeckx (Edinburgh: T. & T. Clark, 1985), 75.

2. W. Seibel, S.J., "Folgen eines Lehrverfahrens," *Stimmen der Zeit* 200 (March, 1980): 145.

3. Ibid. See L. Swidler, "Hans Küng: A Theologian for our Time," *Doctrine and Life* 34 (4, 1984): 179-84.

4. A. Dulles, "The Two Magisteria: An Interim Reflection," *CTSA Proceedings* 35 (1980): 155-69. See K. Rahner, *Theological Investigations XVIII* (New York: Crossroad, 1983), 56-66 and J. Fuchs, "Bischöfe und Moraltheologen: Eine innerkirchliche Spannung," *Stimmen der Zeit* 203 (September, 1983): 601-19.

5. B. Schneider, S.J., "Bemerkungen zur Kritik an der Kirche," *Gott in Welt II: Festgabe für Karl Rahner* (Freiburg: Herder, 1964), 257.

6. M. D. Place, "Theologians and Magisterium from the Council of Trent to the First Vatican Council," *Chicago Studies* 17 (1978): 227.

7. A. Dulles, *Models of the Church* (Garden City, N.Y.: Doubleday, 1974), 40.

8. E. Schillebeeckx, "The Teaching Authority of All—A Reflection about

the Structure of the New Testament," in *The Teaching Authority of the Believers,* 19.

9. Ibid., 21.

10. J. A. Komonchak, "What's happening to doctrine?" *Commonweal* 112 (1985): 457.

11. J. Sobrino, "The 'Doctrinal Authority' of the People of God in Latin America," in *The Teaching Authority of the Believers,* 54-62.

12. E. Schillebeeckx, "The Teaching Authority," 12. See H. Vorgrimler, "From *Sensus Fidei* to *Consensus Fidelium*," in *The Teaching Authority of the Believers,* 3-11.

13. K. Rahner, *Theological Investigations XVIII,* 66.

14. R. J. Penaskovic, *Open To the Spirit: The Notion of the Laity in the Writings of J. H. Newman* (Augsburg: W. Blasaditsch, 1972), 139.

15. K. Rahner, *Free Speech in the Church* (New York: Sheed & Ward, 1959), 22.

16. Ibid., 30.

17. Ibid., 37.

18. H. Mühlen, *Morgen wird Einheit Sein, Das Kommende Konzil aller Christen: Ziel der getrennten Kirchen* (Paderborn: F. Schöningh, 1974), 101.

19. F. Wolfinger, "Die Reception Theologischer Einsichten und Ihre Theologische und Oekumenische Bedeutung: Von der Einsicht zur Verwirklichung," *Catholica* 31 (1977): 204.

20. Duquoc, "An Active Role," 77.

21. Ibid. See H. Fries, "Is There a Magisterium of the Faithful?" in *The Teaching Authority of the Believers,* 82-91.

22. "CTSA Committee Report in Cooperation Between Theologians and the Church's Teaching Authority," *CTSA Proceedings* 35 (1980): 326.

23. Komonchak, 459.

24. T. H. Sanks, S.J., "Co-operation, Co-optation, Condemnation: Theologians and the Magisterium 1970-1978," *Chicago Studies* 17 (2, 1978): 243.

25. Ibid., 247.

26. Ibid., 252.

27. Ibid., 248.

28. K. Rahner, "Open Questions in Dogma Considered by the Institutional Church as Definitively Answered," *JES* 15 (1978): 226.

29. Ibid., 215.

30. J. E. Thiel, "Orthodoxy and Heterodoxy in Schleiermacher's Theological Encyclopedia: Doctrinal Development and Theological Creativity," *HJ* 25 (1984): 157.

31. Ibid.

32. Komonchak, 459.

33. Dulles, "The Two Magisteria," 168.

34. B. Häring, "The Encyclical Crisis," *Commonweal* 80 (1961): 588-94.

35. A. M. Greeley, "What is Subsidiarity? A Voice from Sleepy Hollow," *America* 153 (1985): 292.

36. A. Dulles, "Authority: The Divided Legacy," *Commonweal* 12 (1985): 402.

37. J. Heft, "Episcopal Teaching Authority on Matters of War and Economics," ch. 8 of this book.

38. Place, 239.

39. Fuchs, 606.

40. K. Rahner, S.J., "Theologie und Lehramt," *Stimmen Der Zeit* 200 (1980): 343.

41. Fuchs, 616ff.

42. K. Rahner, *Grace in Freedom* (New York: Herder & Herder, 1969) 176.

43. R. A. McCormick argues that the church cannot expect theologians to assent to moral formulations which they judge to be erroneous. The human mind can assent to what it perceives to be true in itself or it can assent because of trust in the teacher. Neither of these can occur if there are contrary reasons utterly persuasive to an individual. See "L' Affaire Curran." *America* 154 (1986): 264.

44. Rahner, "Theologie und Lehramt," 374.

45. Ibid., 370.